T5-CQB-590

Love Songs of the '40s & '50s

ISBN 0-7935-8341-1

HAL•LEONARD® CORPORATION

7777 W. BLUEMOUND RD. P.O. BOX 13819 MILWAUKEE, WI 53213

Visit Hal Leonard Online at
www.halleonard.com

Contents

ALL OF YOU
from SILK STOCKINGS

Words and Music by
COLE PORTER

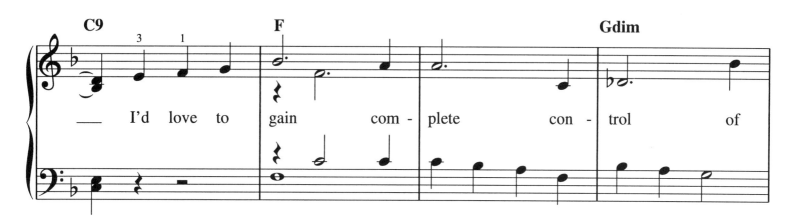

I'd love to gain com-plete con-trol of

you, And han-dle e-ven the heart and soul of

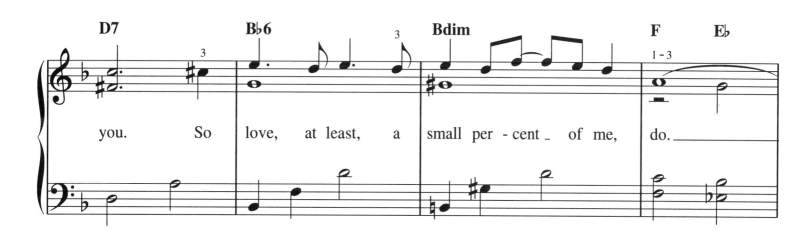

you. So love, at least, a small per-cent of me, do.

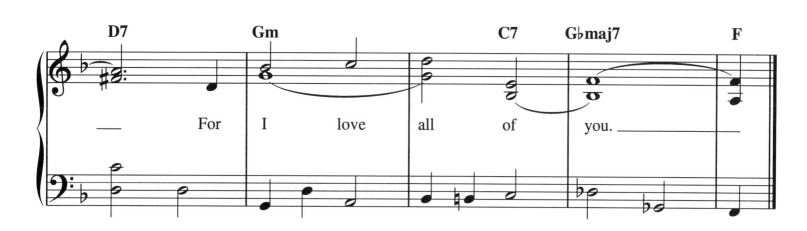

For I love all of you.

ALWAYS IN MY HEART
(Siempre En Mi Corazon)

English Lyric by KIM GANNON
Original Words and Music by ERNESTO LECUONA

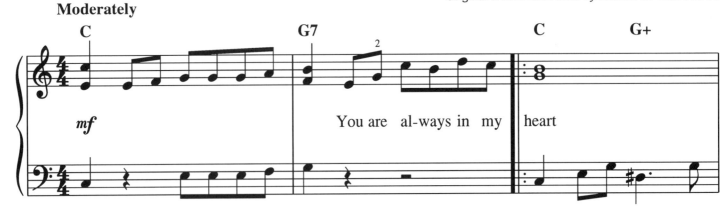

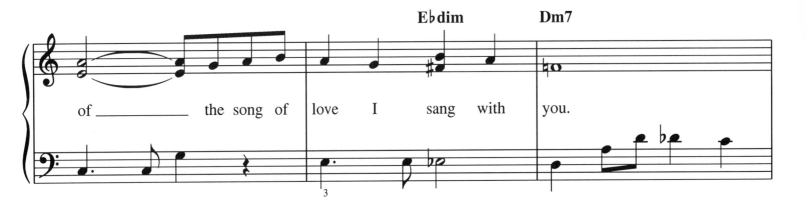

grey, I re-mem-ber that you care _____ and then and

there the sun breaks through. Just be-fore I go to

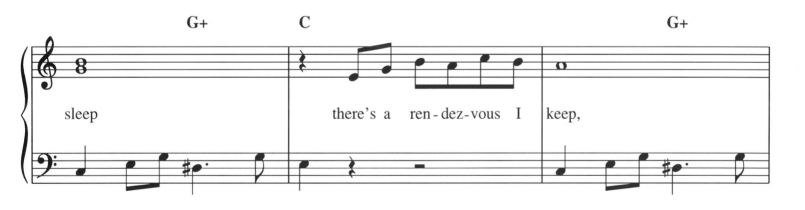

sleep there's a ren-dez-vous I keep,

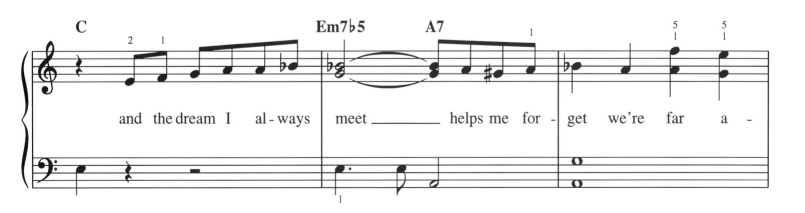

and the dream I al-ways meet _____ helps me for - get we're far a-

8

Dm

part.

Dm7♭5

I don't know ex - act - ly | when   dear,

Fm

but I'm sure we'll meet a - | gain,   dear,

C

Eb dim

and, my dar - ling, till we

G7

do

1.

C

you are al - ways in my | heart.

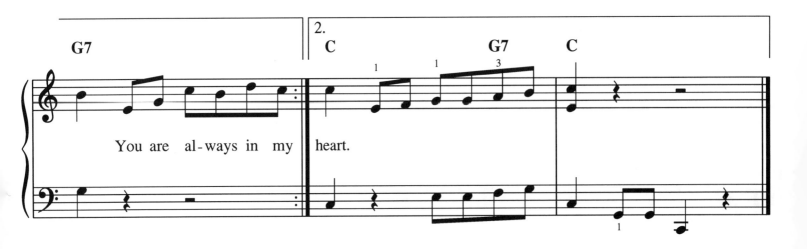

G7

You are al - ways in my | heart.

2.

C

G7   C

BEWITCHED

from PAL JOEY

Words by LORENZ HART
Music by RICHARD RODGERS

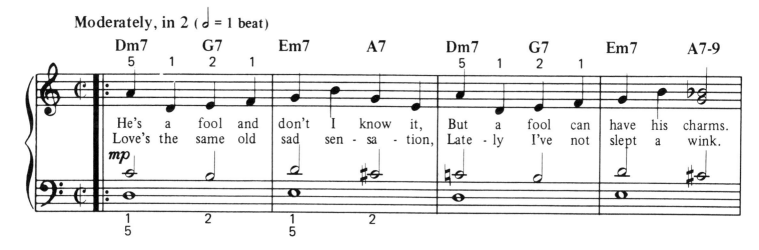

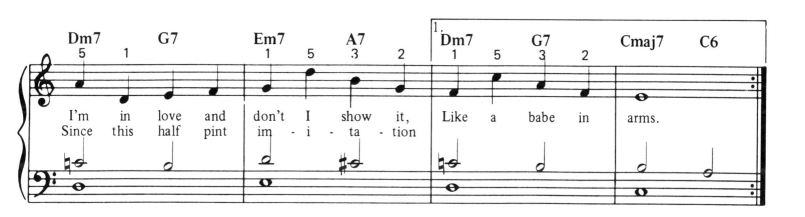

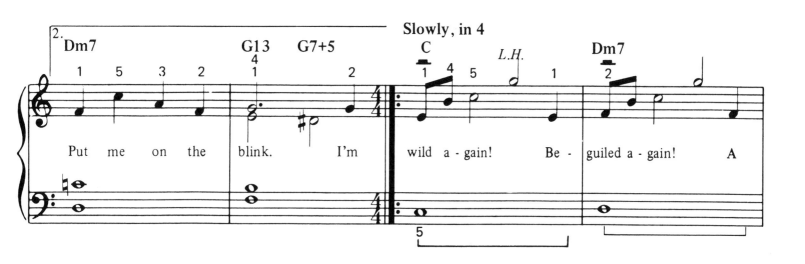

simp-er-ing, whimp-er-ing child a - gain. Be - witched, both-ered and be - wil - dered am

Could-n't sleep And would-n't sleep When

love came and told me I should-n't sleep. Be - witched, both-ered and be- wil - dered am

Lost my heart, but what of it?

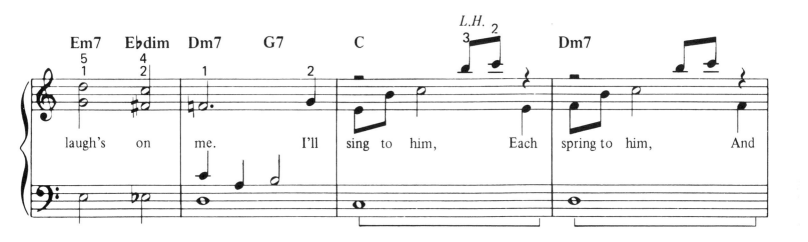

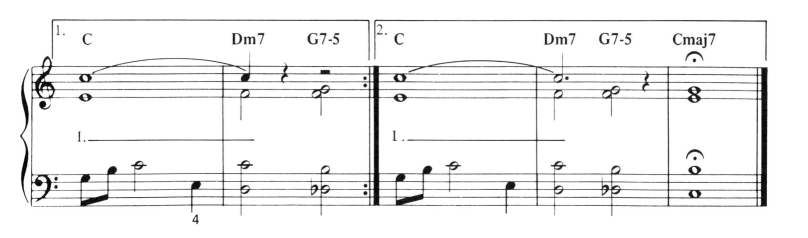

AND THIS IS MY BELOVED

from KISMET

Words and Music by ROBERT WRIGHT
and GEORGE FORREST
(Music Based on Themes of A. BORODIN)

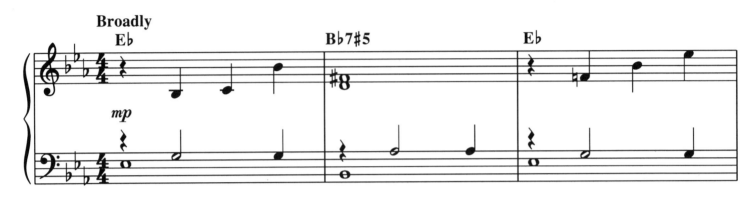

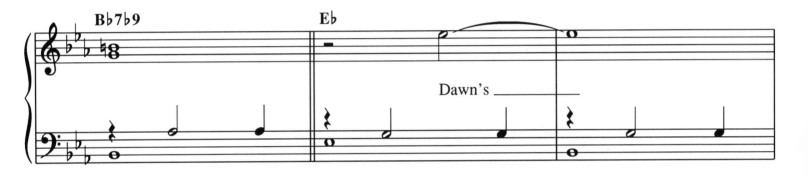

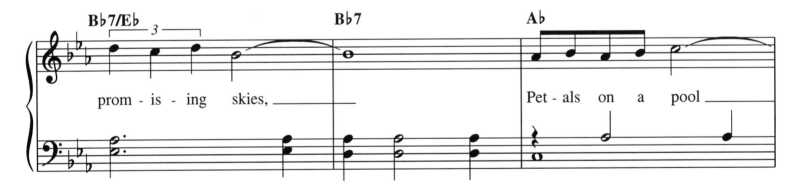

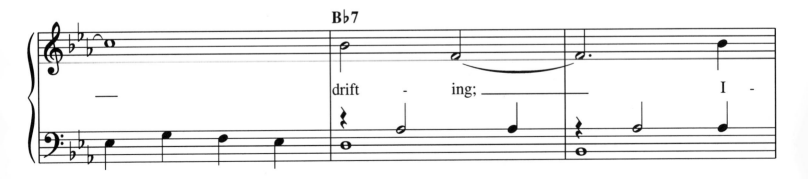

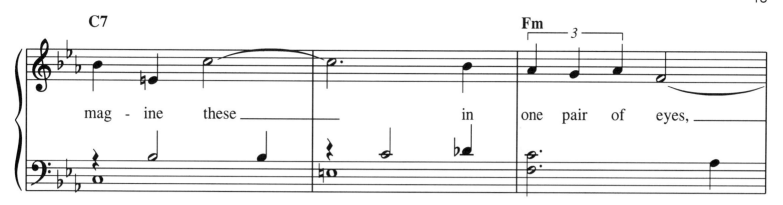

mag - ine these _____ in one pair of eyes, _____

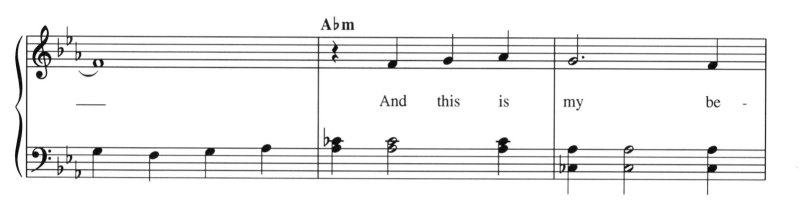

_____ And this is my be -

lov - ed. _____ Strange _____

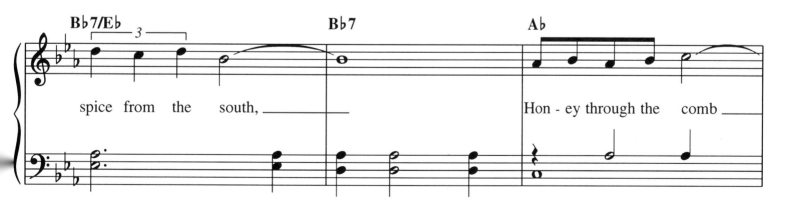

spice from the south, _____ Hon - ey through the comb _____

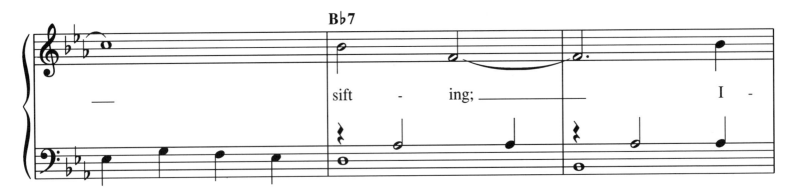

sift - ing; _____ I -

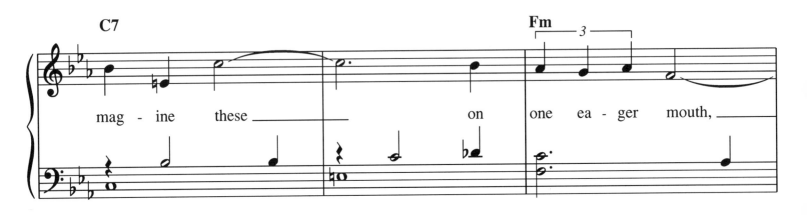

mag - ine these _____ on one ea - ger mouth, _____

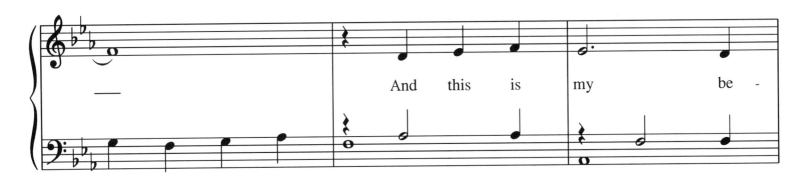

_____ And this is my be -

lov - ed. _____ And when { she / he }

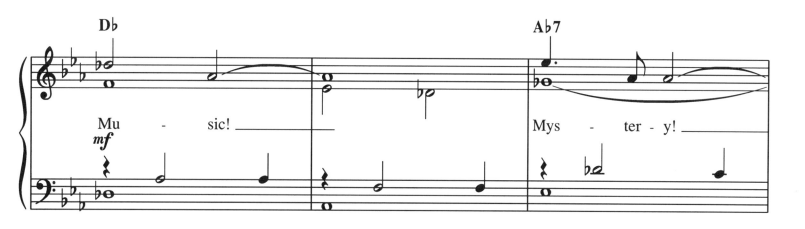

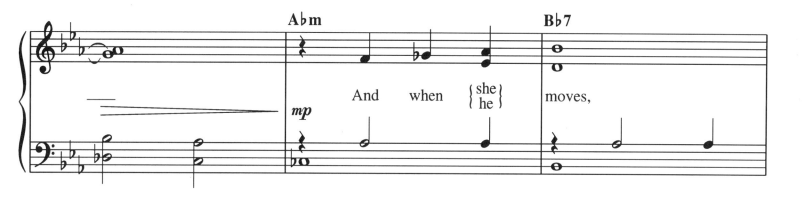

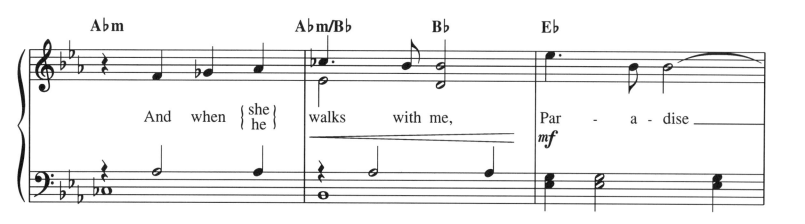

15

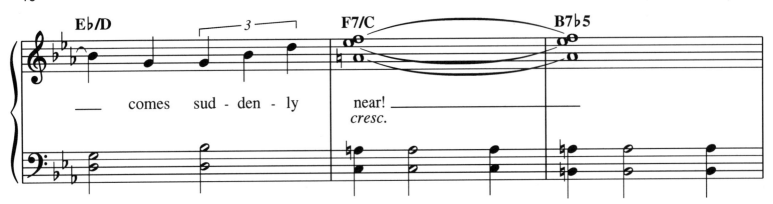

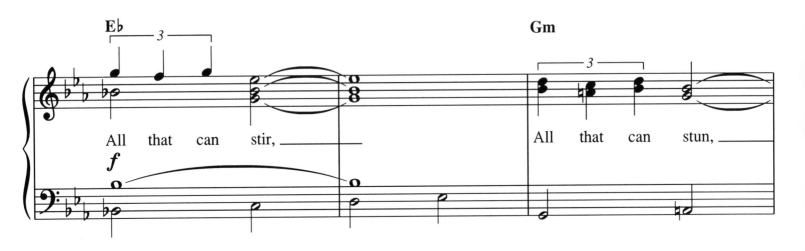

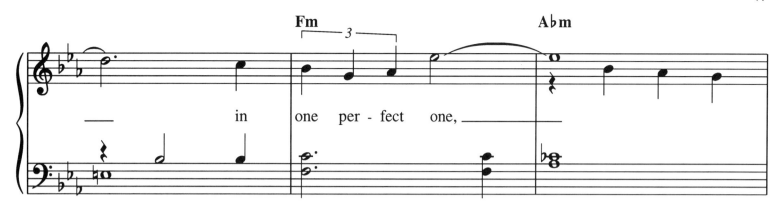

in one per-fect one, _____

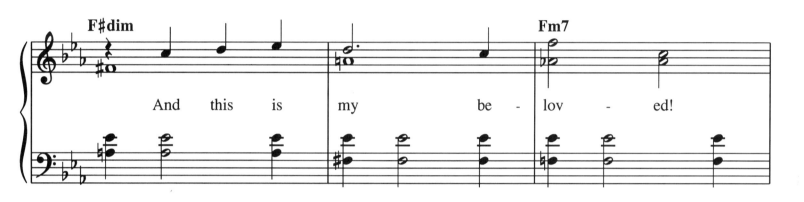

And this is my be - lov - ed!

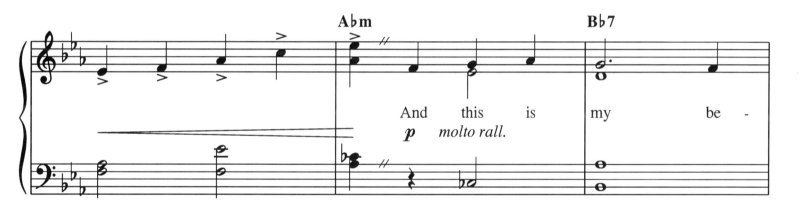

And this is my be -

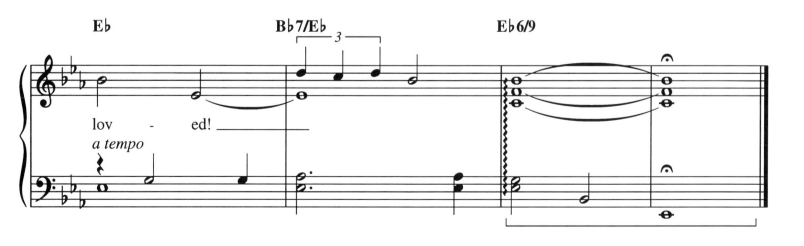

lov - ed! _____

ANNIVERSARY SONG

from the Columbia Picture THE JOLSON STORY

By AL JOLSON
and SAUL CHAPLIN

Moderately slow

With pedal

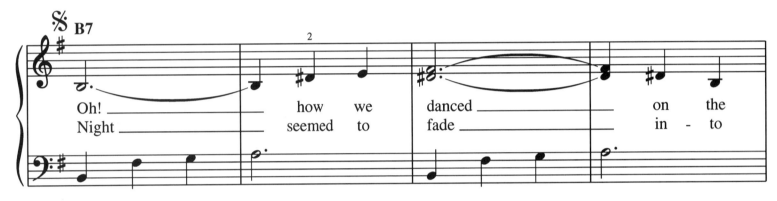

Oh! _____ how we danced _____ on the
Night _____ seemed to fade _____ in - to

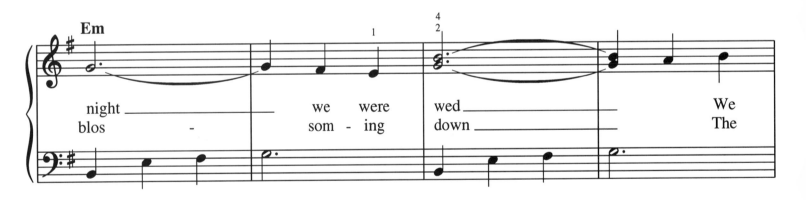

night _____ we were wed _____ We
blos - som - ing down _____ The

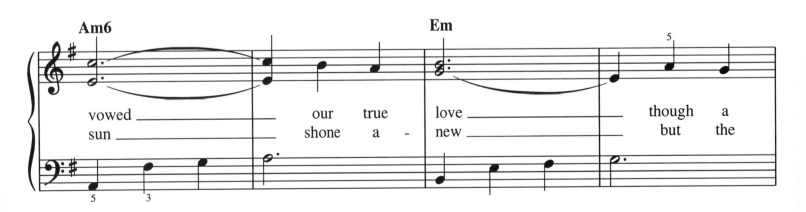

vowed _____ our true love _____ though a
sun _____ shone a - new _____ but the

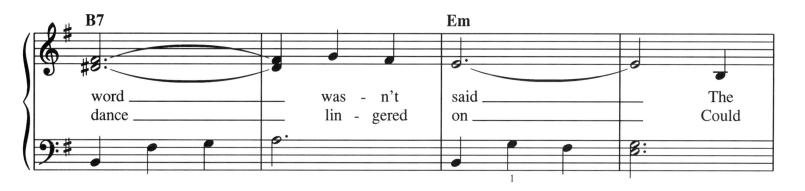

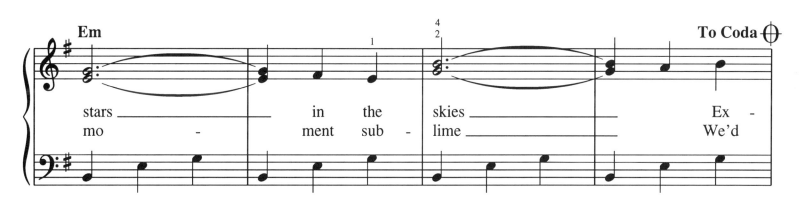

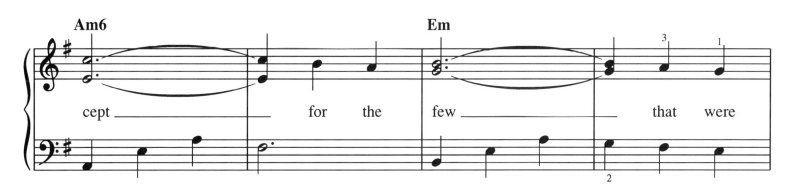

20

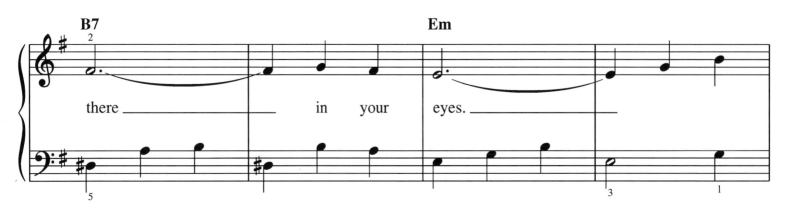

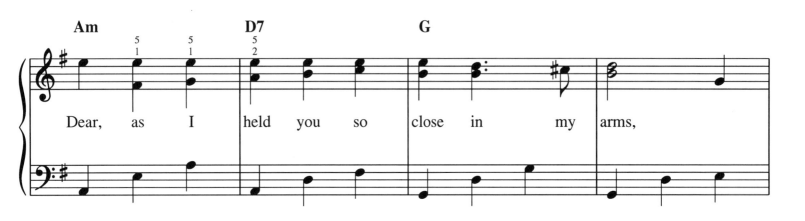

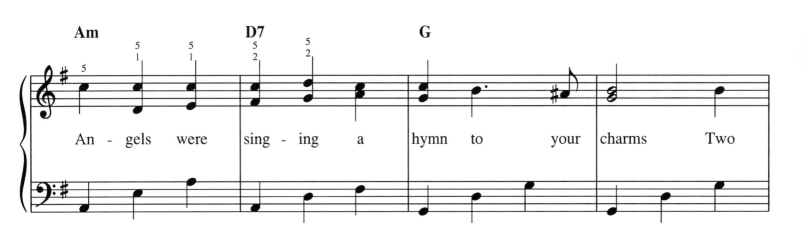

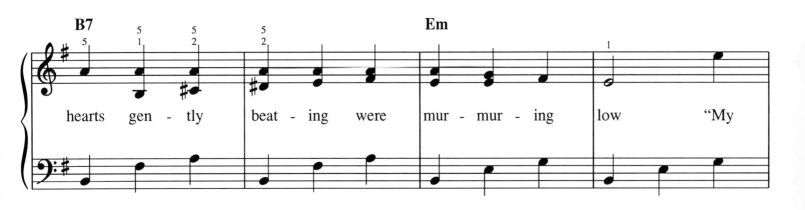

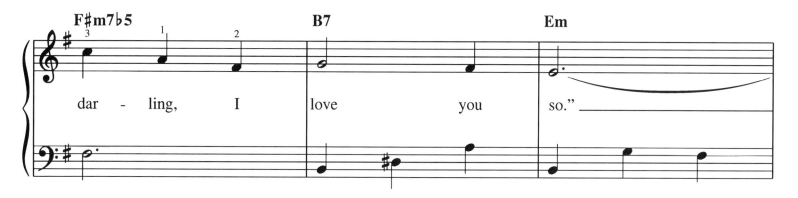

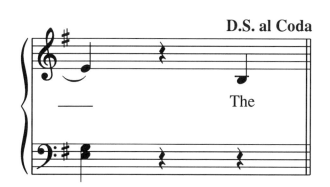

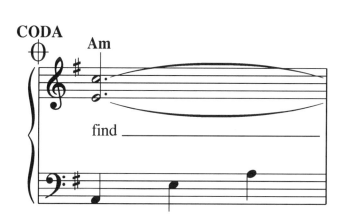

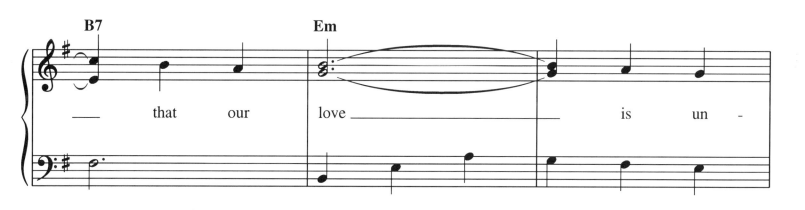

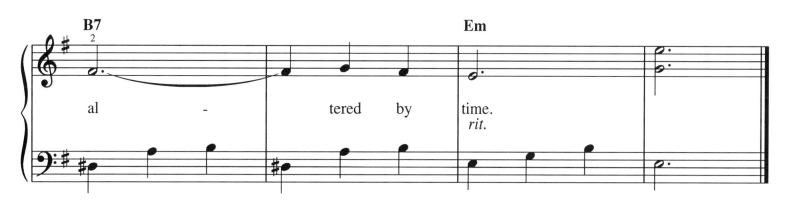

THE ANNIVERSARY WALTZ

Words and Music by AL DUBIN
and DAVE FRANKLIN

23

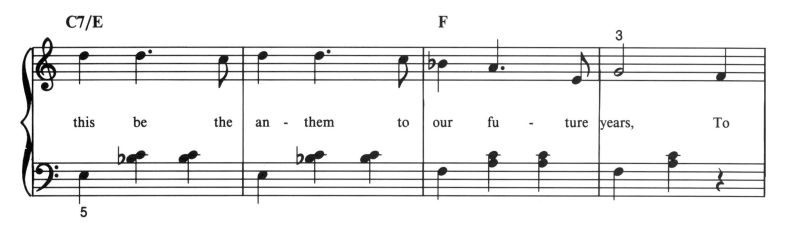

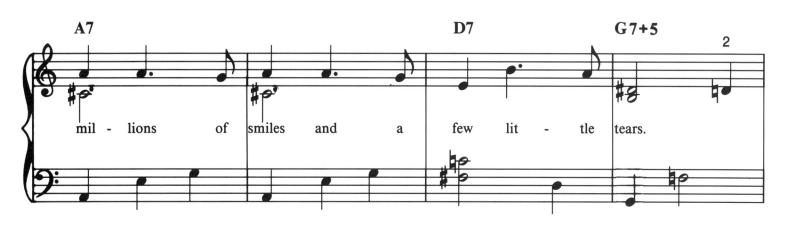

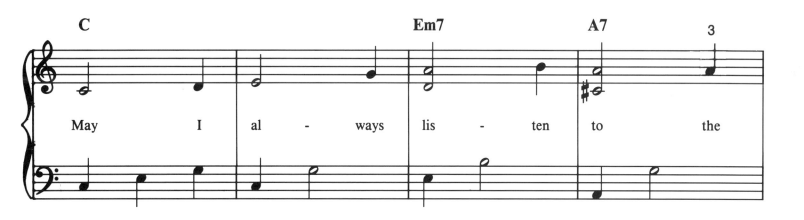

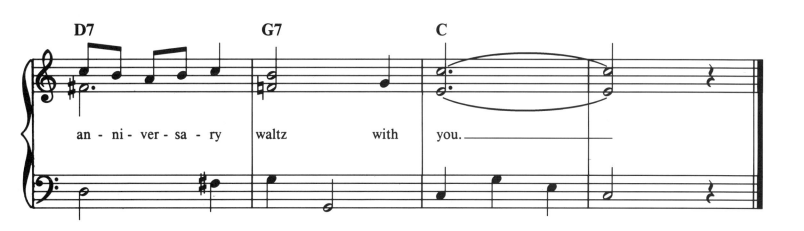

AROUND THE WORLD

from AROUND THE WORLD IN EIGHTY DAYS

Words and Music by VICTOR YOUNG
and HAROLD ADAMSON

Fast Waltz (in 1)

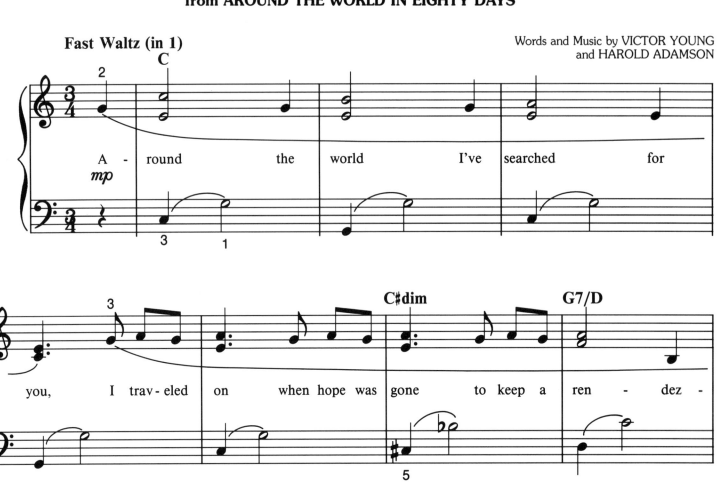

A - round the world I've searched for you, I trav-eled on when hope was gone to keep a ren - dez -

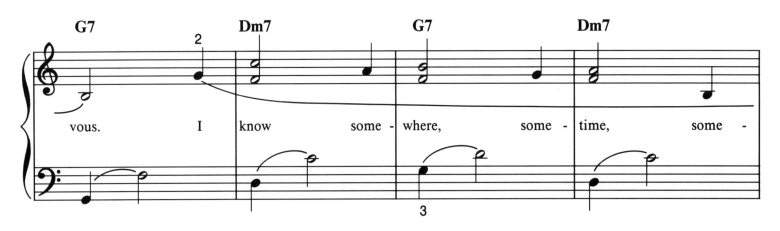

vous. I know some - where, some - time, some -

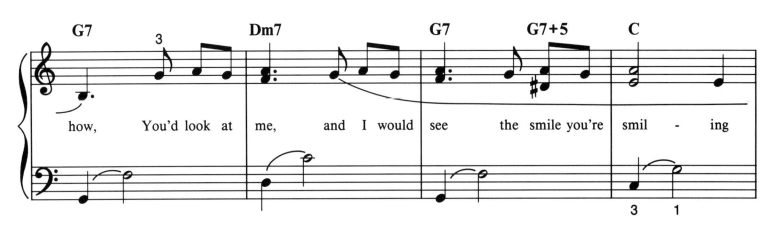

how, You'd look at me, and I would see the smile you're smil - ing

25

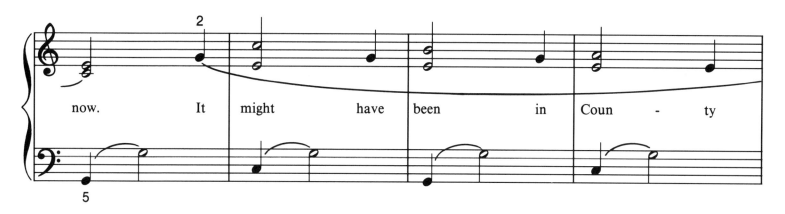

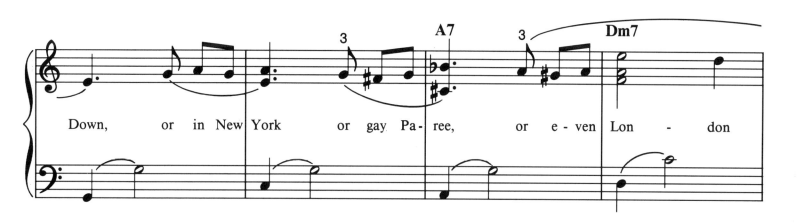

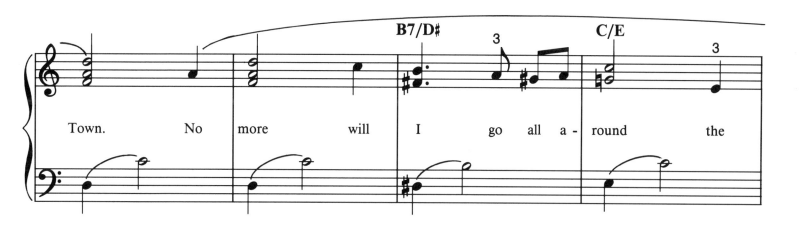

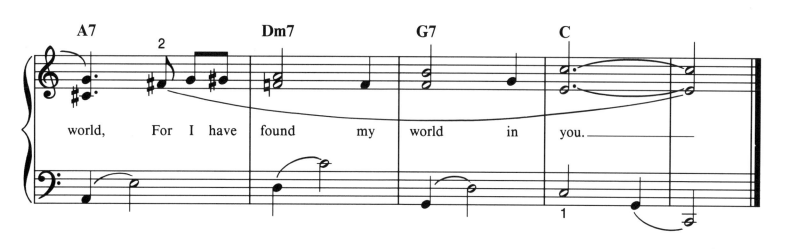

BÈSAME MUCHO
(Kiss Me Much)

English Lyric by SUNNY SKYLAR
Music and Spanish Lyric by CONSUELO VELAZQUEZ

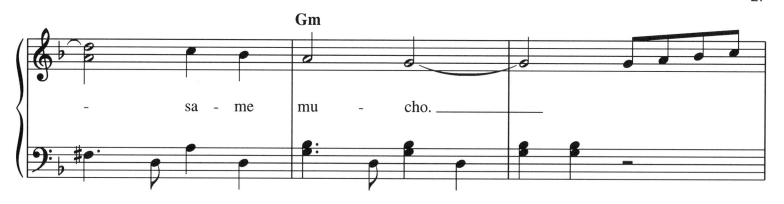

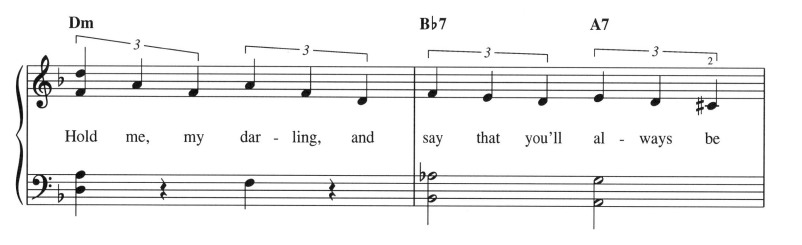

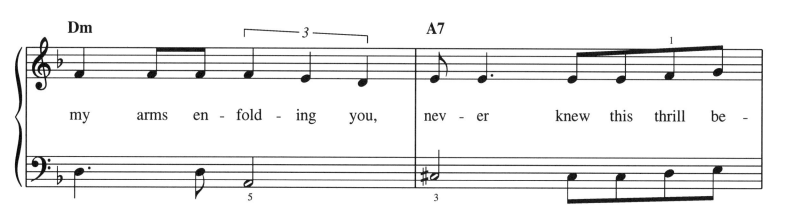

fore. Who ev - er thought I'd be hold - ing you close to me,

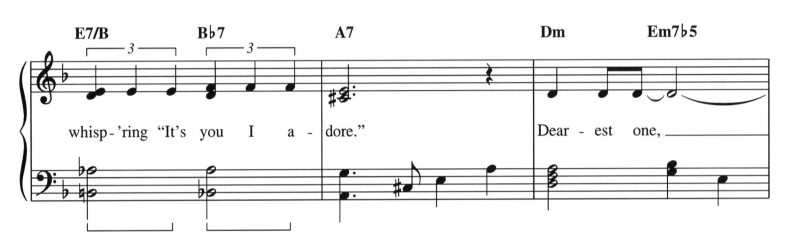

whisp - 'ring "It's you I a - dore." Dear - est one, ___

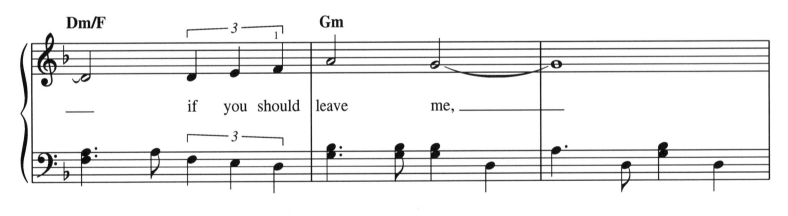

___ if you should leave me, ___

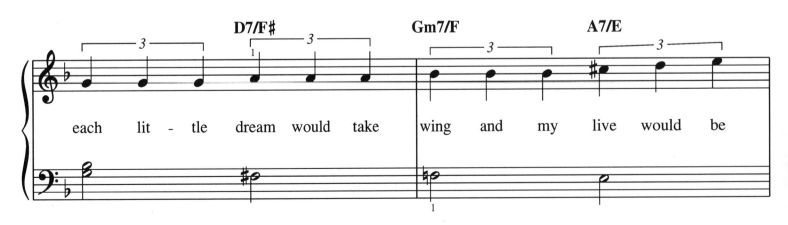

each lit - tle dream would take wing and my live would be

through.   Be -

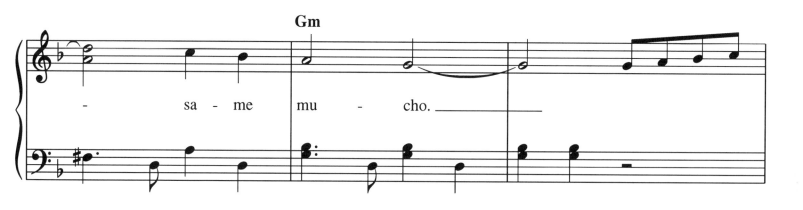

- sa - me mu - cho. _____

Love me for - ev - er   and make all my   dreams _ come true.

true.

C'EST SI BON
(It's So Good)

English Words by JERRY SEELEN
French Words by ANDRE HORNEZ
Music by HENRI BETTI

MCA music publishing

you, _____ like the French peo-p' do, _____ be-cause it's oh, so

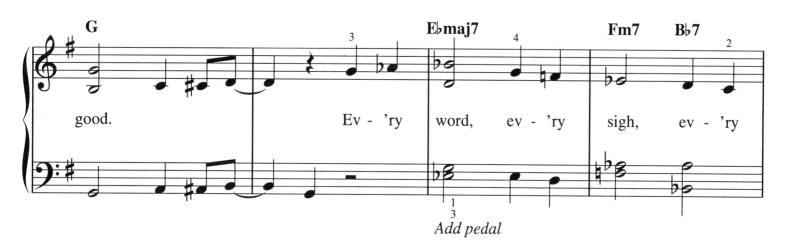

good. Ev - 'ry word, ev - 'ry sigh, ev - 'ry

Add pedal

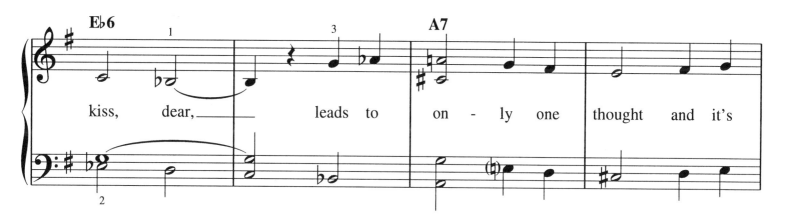

kiss, dear, _____ leads to on - ly one thought and it's

this, dear. It's so good, _____ noth-ing else can re -

No pedal

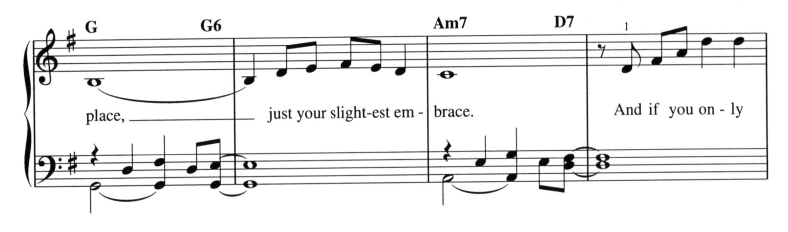

place, _____ just your slight-est em - brace. And if you on - ly

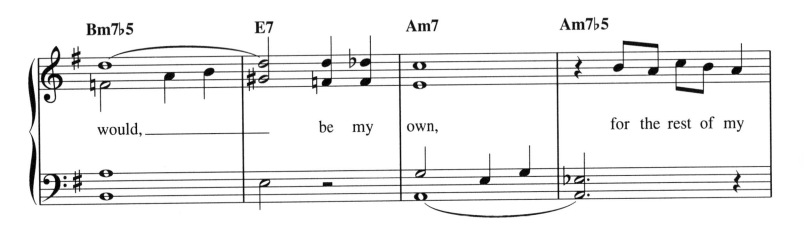

would, _____ be my own, for the rest of my

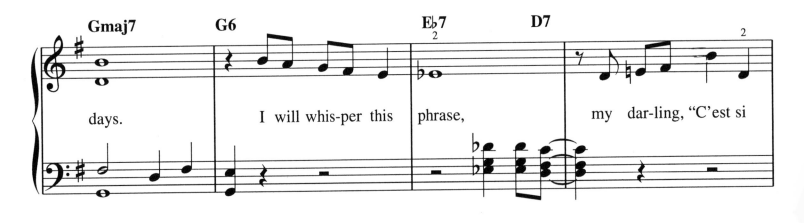

days. I will whis-per this phrase, my dar-ling, "C'est si

1.
bon." "C'est si

2.
bon."

CHANSON D'AMOUR
(The Ra-Da-Da-Da-Da Song)

Words and Music by
WAYNE SHANKLIN

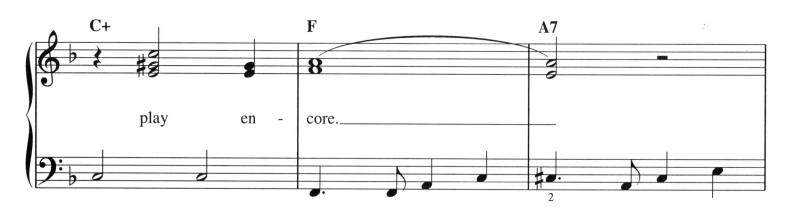

Here in my heart ra da da da

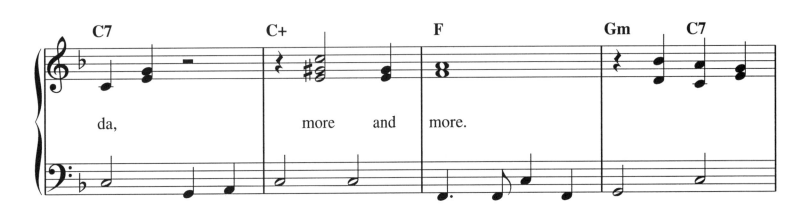

da, more and more.

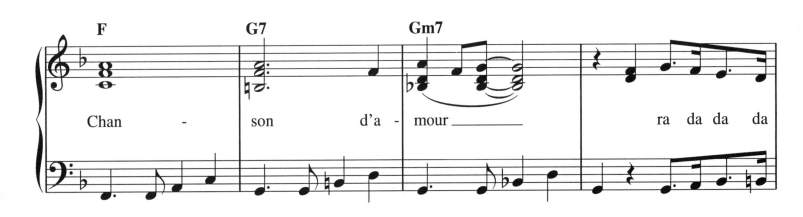

Chan - son d'a - mour _____ ra da da da

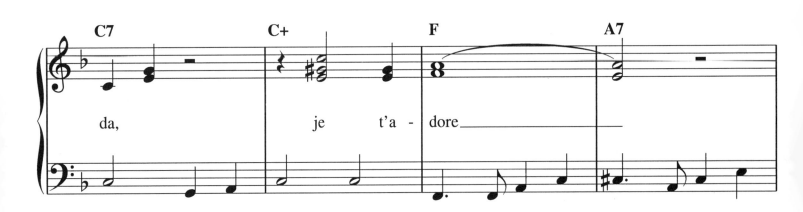

da, je t'a - dore _____

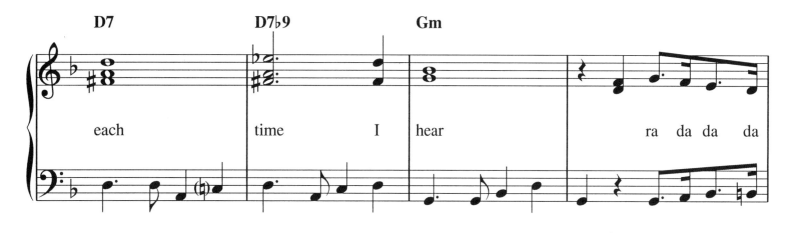

each time I hear ra da da da

da chan-son,__ chan - son d'a mour.

1.
F
2
1
C7

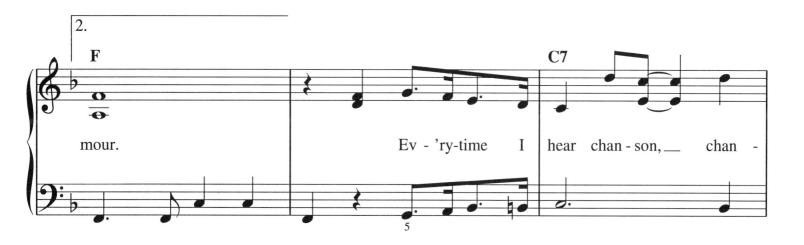

2.
F

mour. Ev - 'ry-time I hear chan - son,__ chan -

C7

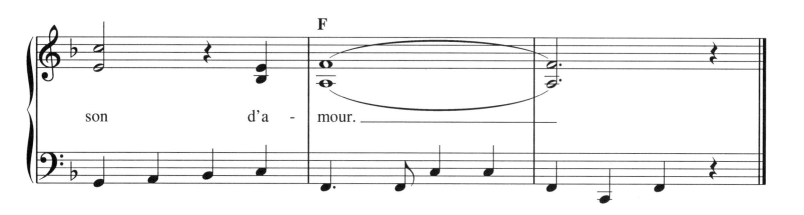

son d'a - mour. _____

F

CLOSE AS PAGES IN A BOOK
from UP IN CENTRAL PARK

Words by DOROTHY FIELDS
Music by SIGMUND ROMBERG

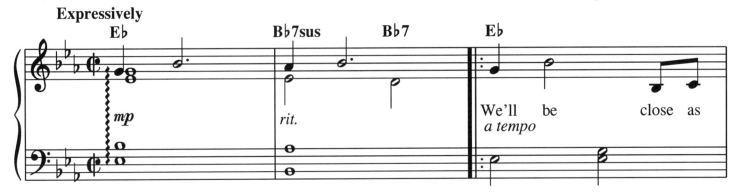

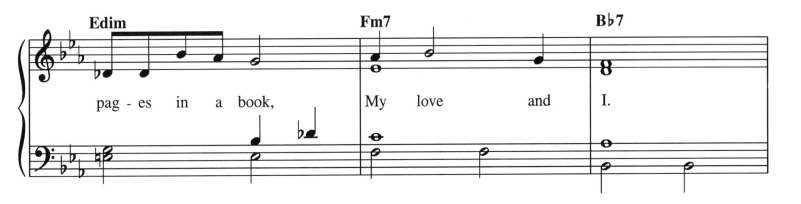

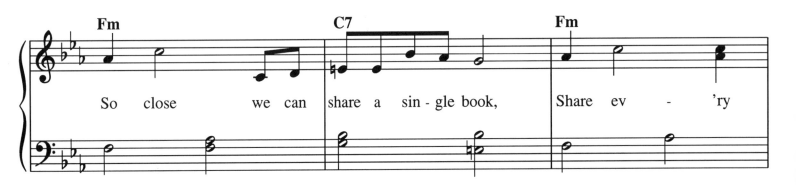

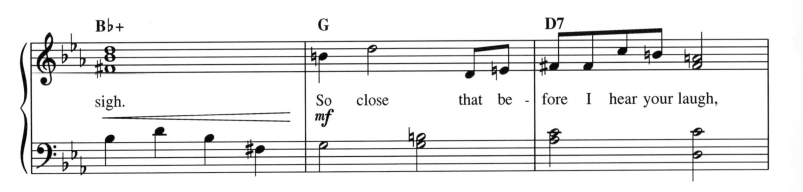

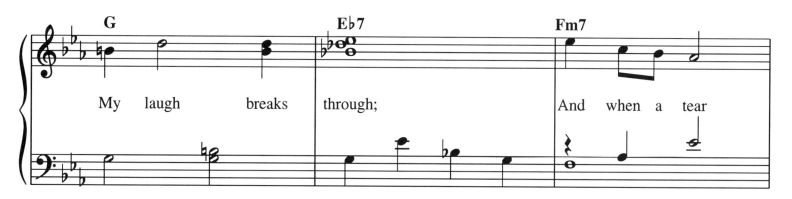

My laugh breaks through; And when a tear

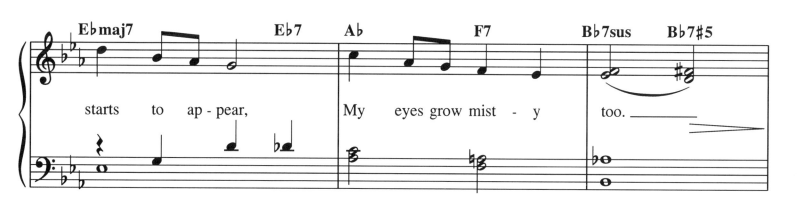

starts to ap - pear, My eyes grow mist - y too. _____

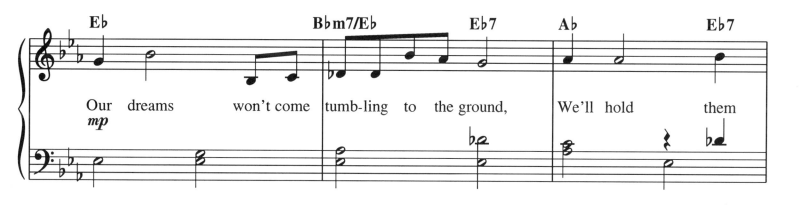

Our dreams won't come tumb-ling to the ground, We'll hold them
mp

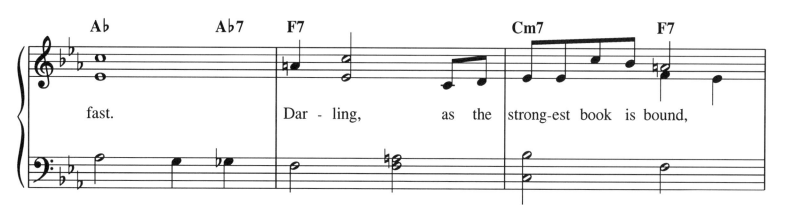

fast. Dar - ling, as the strong-est book is bound,

We're bound to last. Your life is

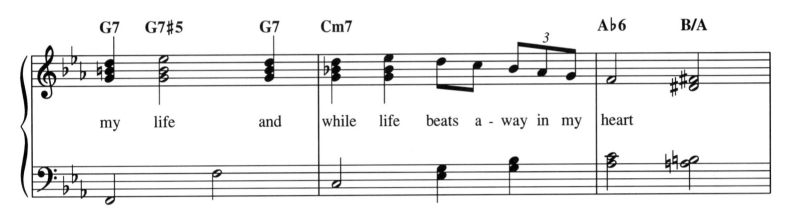

my life and while life beats a - way in my heart

We'll be close as pag - es in a book, Nev - er to

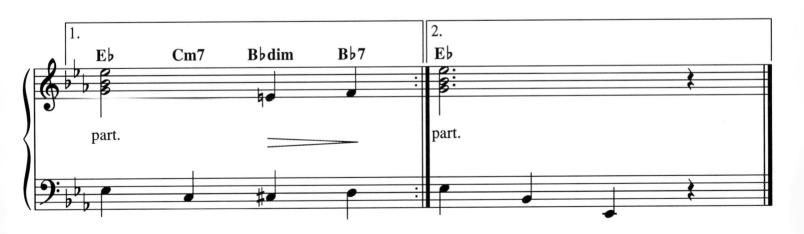

part. part.

DAY BY DAY
Theme from the Paramount Television Series DAY BY DAY

Words and Music by SAMMY CAHN,
AXEL STORDAHL and PAUL WESTON

Slowly with expression

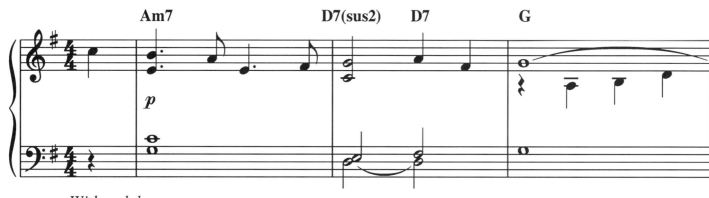

With pedal

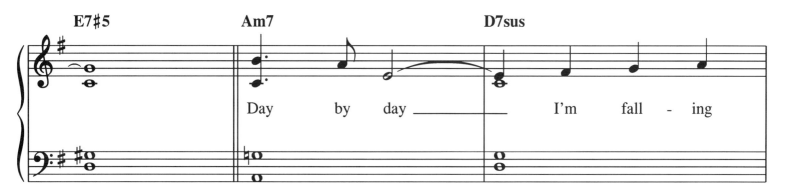

Day by day _____ I'm fall - ing

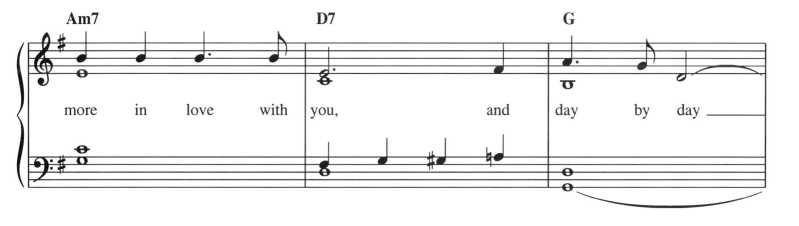

more in love with you, and day by day _____

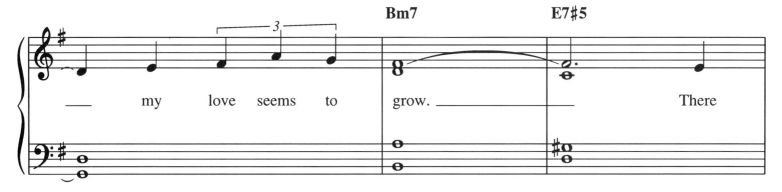

_____ my love seems to grow. _____ There

40

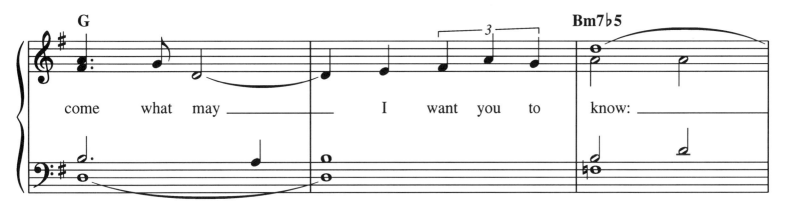

come what may ____ I want you to know: ____

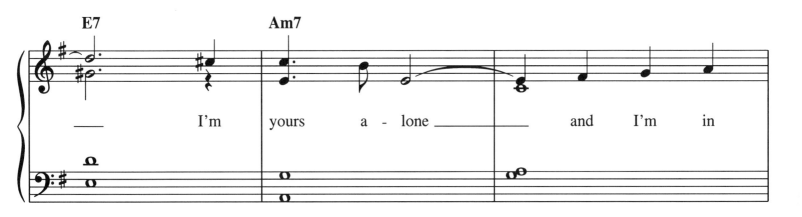

____ I'm yours a - lone ____ and I'm in

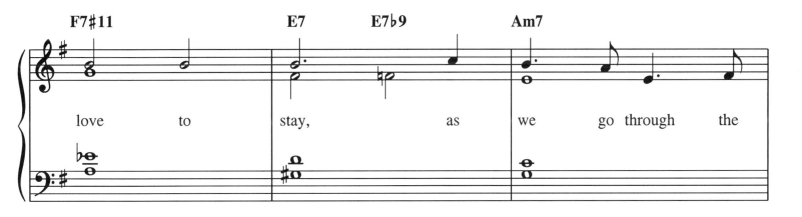

love to stay, as we go through the

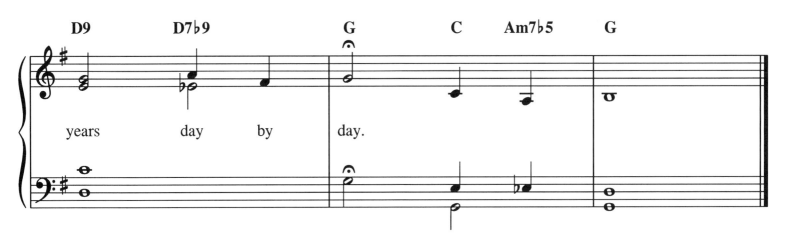

years day by day.

DEARLY BELOVED

from YOU WERE NEVER LOVELIER

Music by JEROME KERN
Words by JOHNNY MERCER

Dear - ly be - lov - ed, how clear - ly I see some - where in heav - en you were fash - ioned for me.

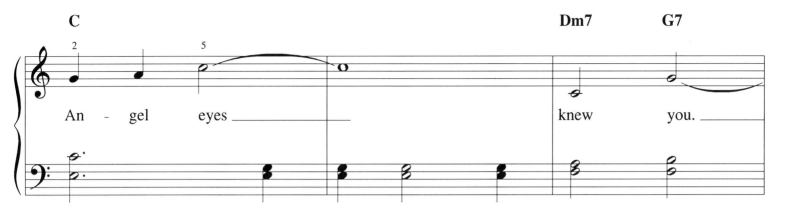

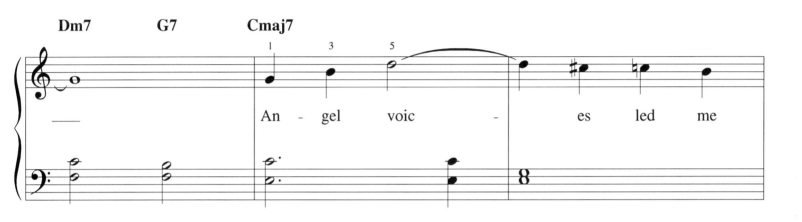

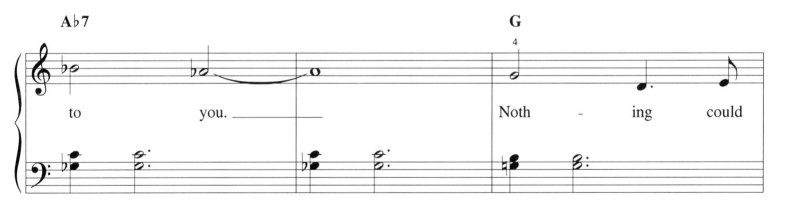

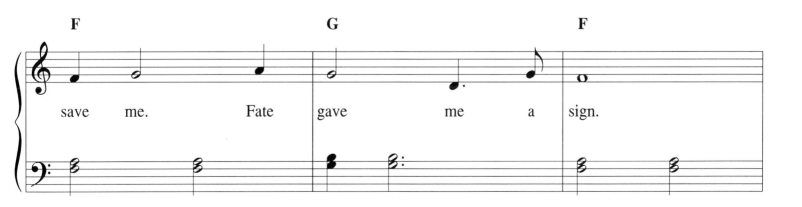

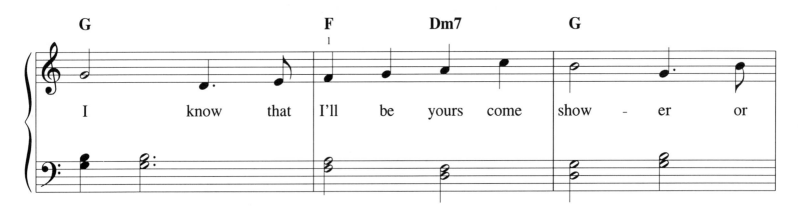

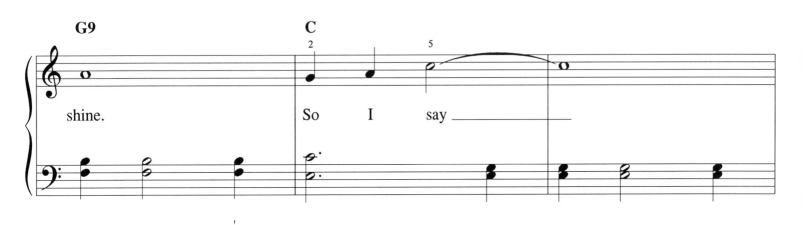

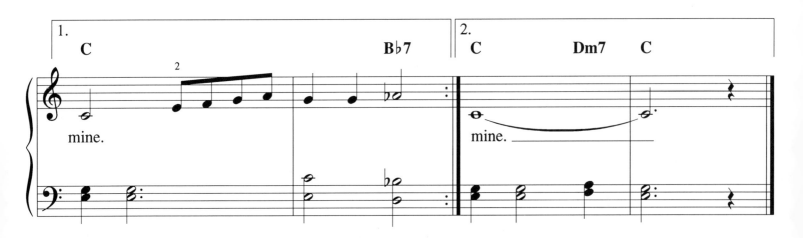

DO I LOVE YOU BECAUSE YOU'RE BEAUTIFUL?

from CINDERELLA

Lyrics by OSCAR HAMMERSTEIN II
Music by RICHARD RODGERS

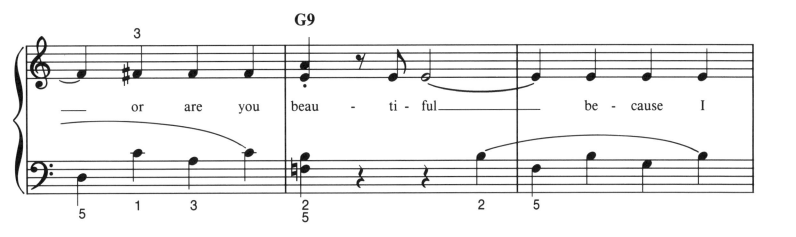

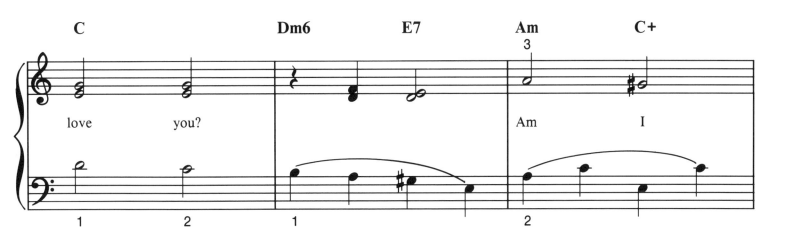

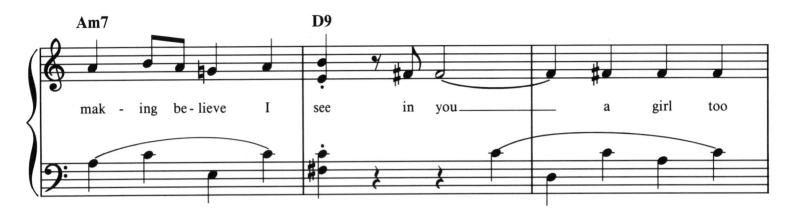

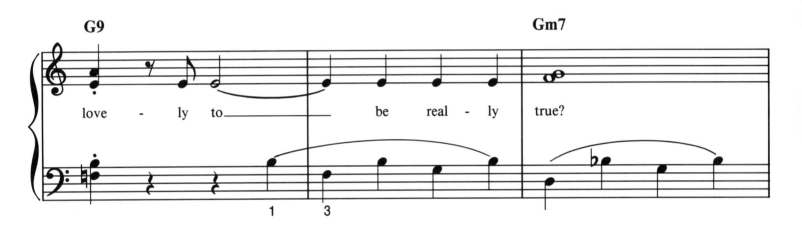

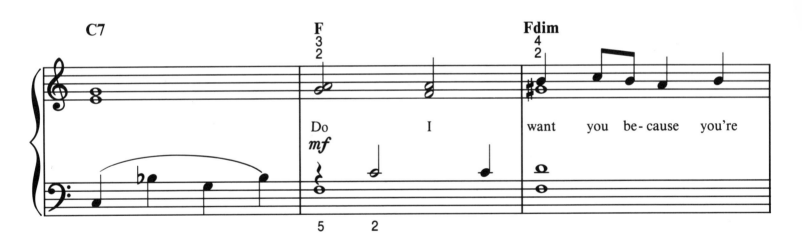

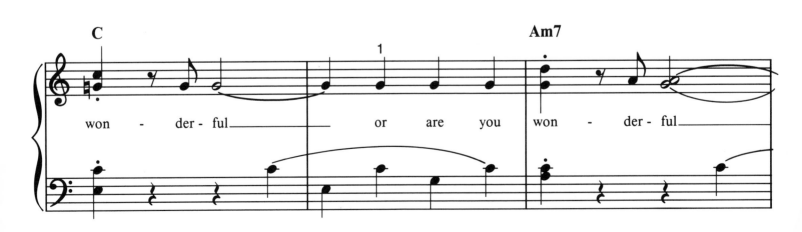

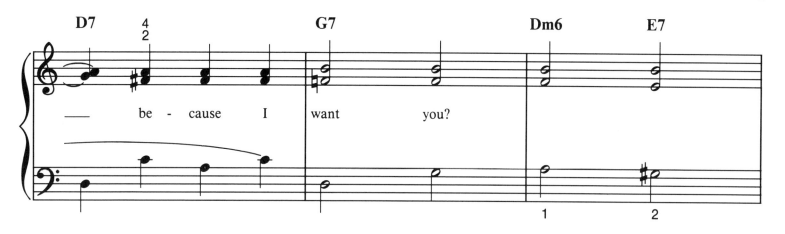

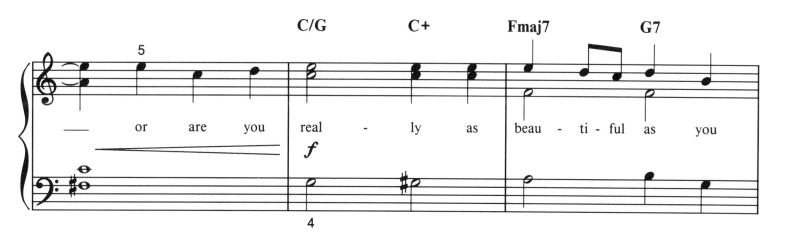

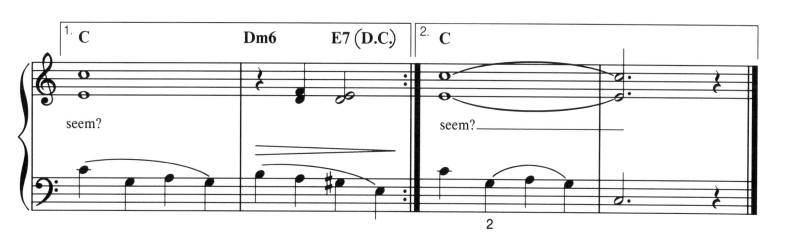

DO NOTHIN' TILL YOU HEAR FROM ME

Words and Music by BOB RUSSELL
and DUKE ELLINGTON

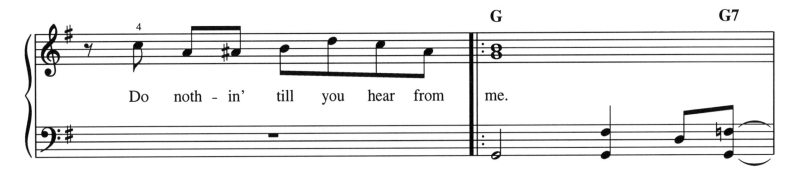

Do noth-in' till you hear from me.

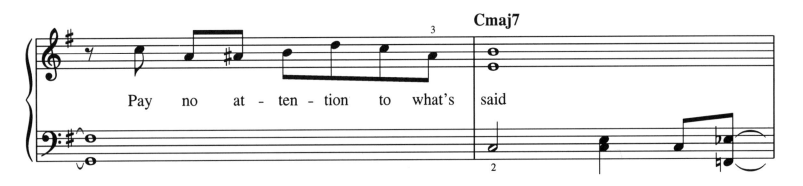

Pay no at-ten-tion to what's said

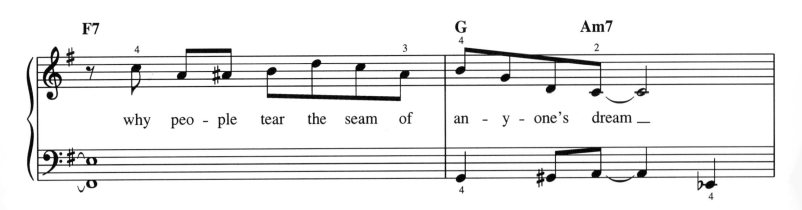

why peo-ple tear the seam of an-y-one's dream

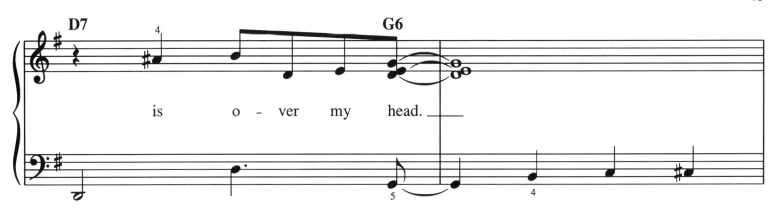

is o - ver my head. ___

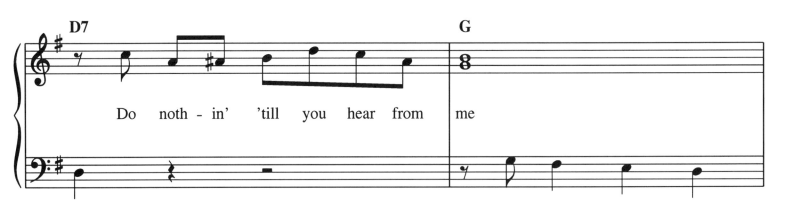

Do noth - in' 'till you hear from me

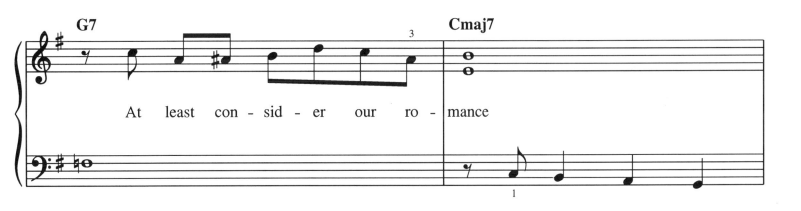

At least con - sid - er our ro - mance

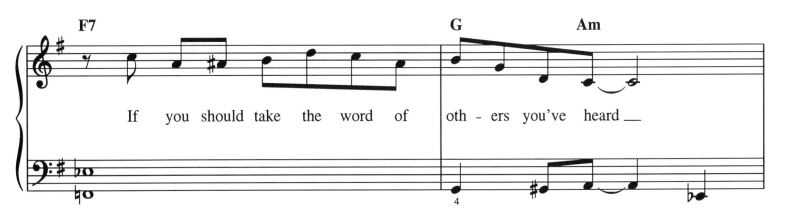

If you should take the word of oth - ers you've heard ___

50

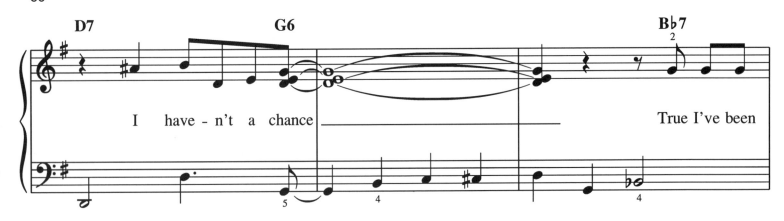

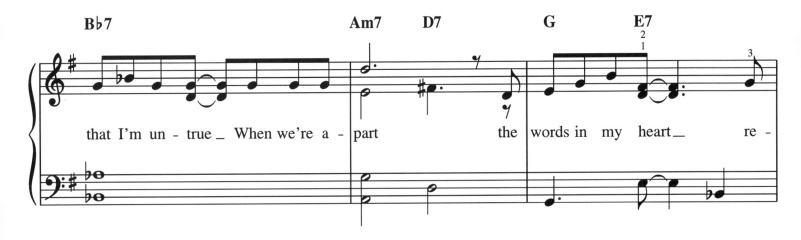

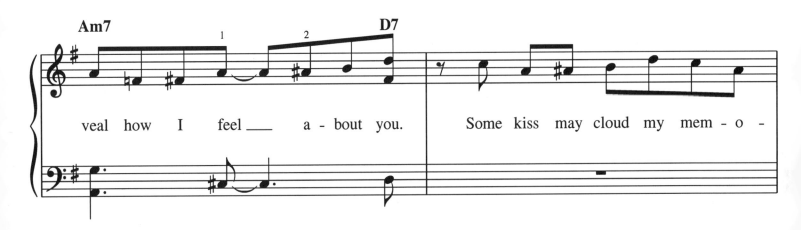

51

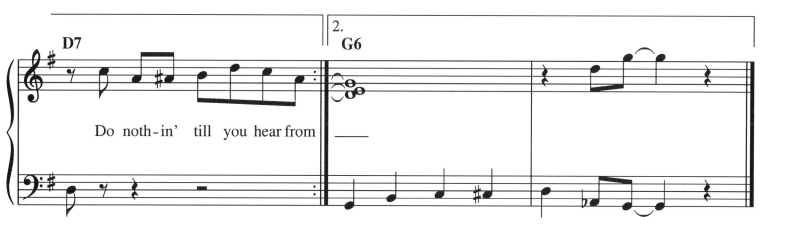

EV'RY TIME WE SAY GOODBYE

from SEVEN LIVELY ARTS

Words and Music by
COLE PORTER

FLY ME TO THE MOON
(In Other Words)
featured in the Motion Picture ONCE AROUND

Words and Music by
BART HOWARD

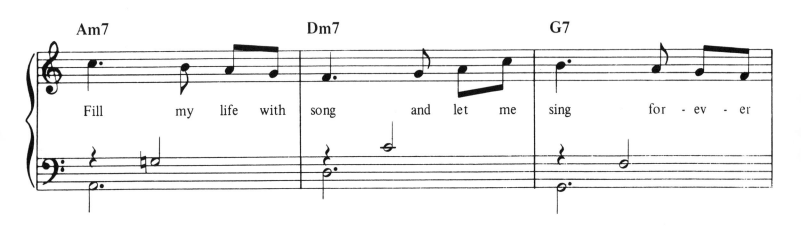

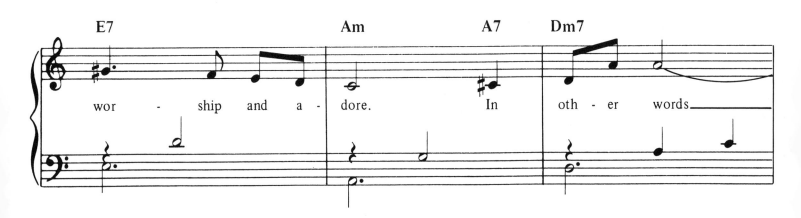

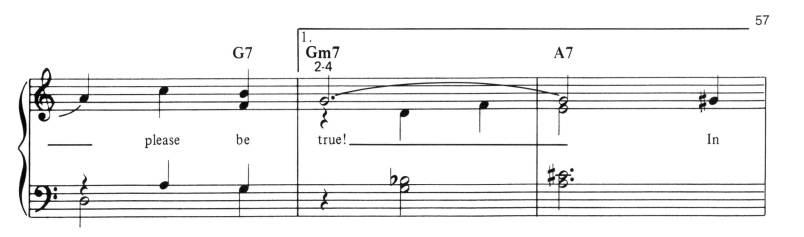
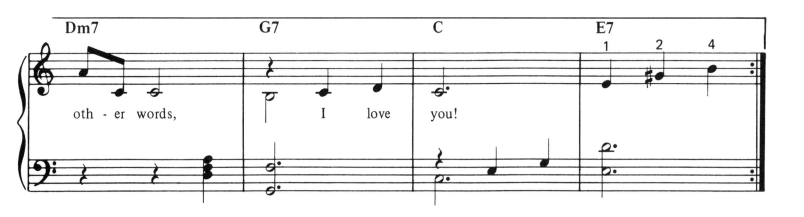
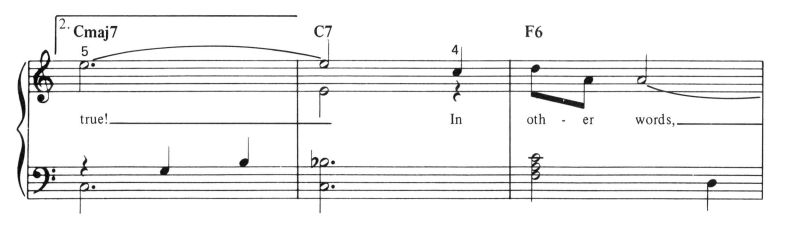
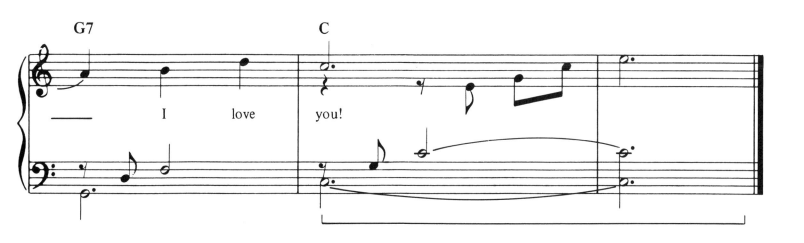

(I Love You)
FOR SENTIMENTAL REASONS

Words by DEEK WATSON
Music by WILLIAM BEST

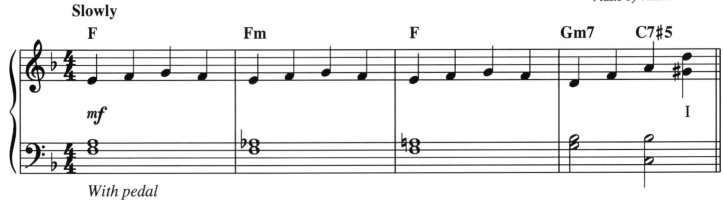

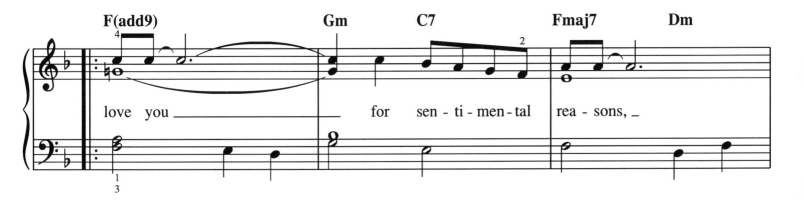

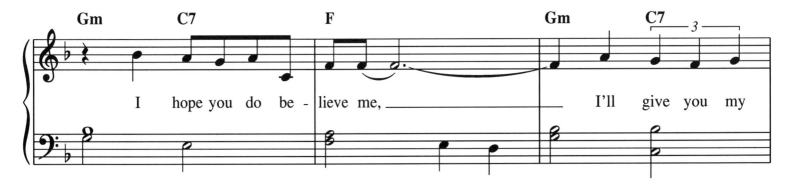

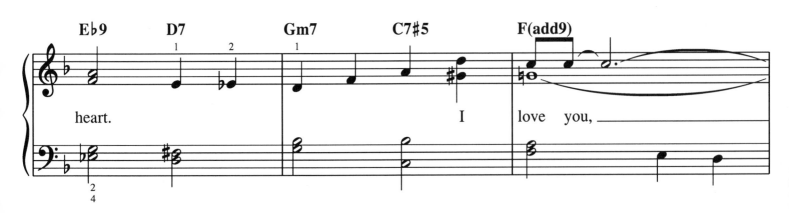

MCA music publishing

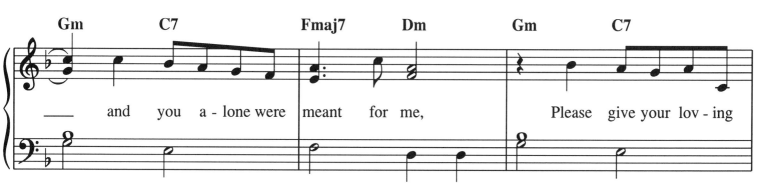

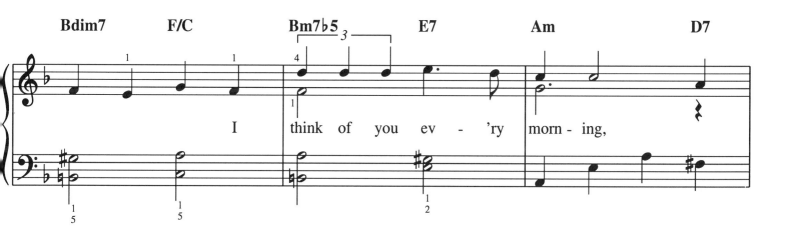

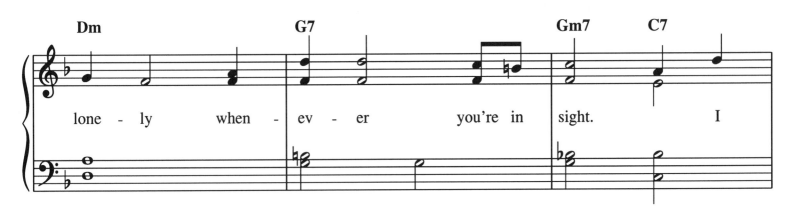

lone - ly when - ev - er you're in sight. I

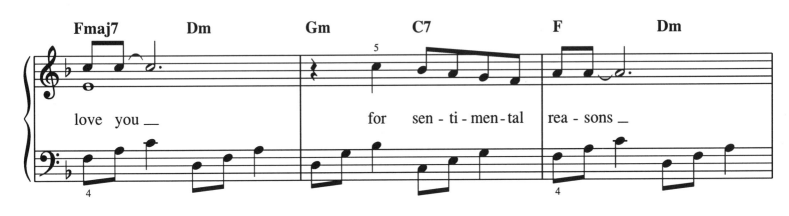

love you __ for sen - ti - men - tal rea - sons __

I have you do be - lieve me, __ I've giv - en you my

heart. I heart. *rit.*

THE GREAT PRETENDER

Words and Music by
BUCK RAM

Moderately slow

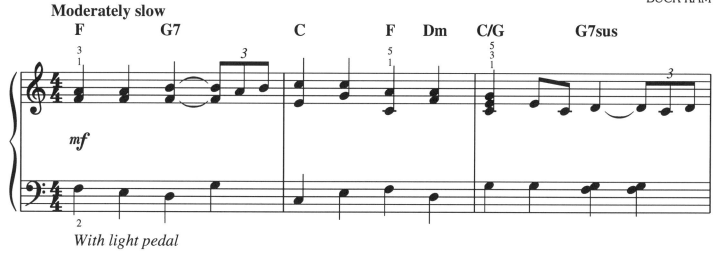

mf

With light pedal

Oh, yes ___ I'm the great pre - tend - er, ___ pre -

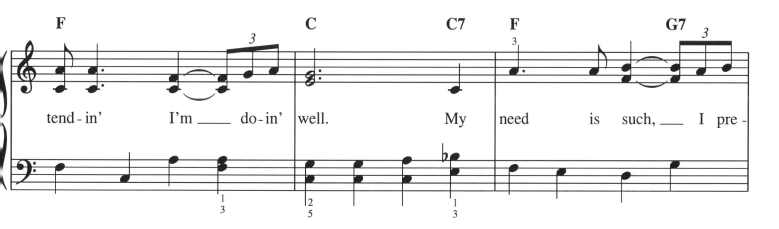

tend - in' I'm ___ do - in' well. My need is such, ___ I pre -

tend too much, I'm lone - ly but no ___ one can tell. Oh,

62

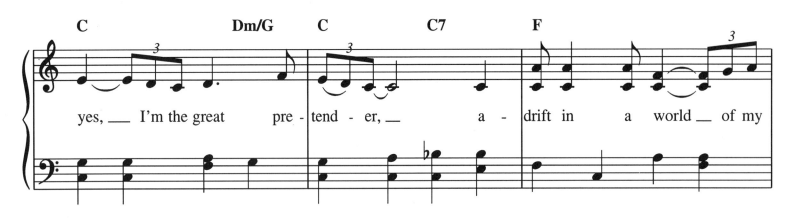

yes, __ I'm the great pre-tend - er, __ a - drift in a world __ of my

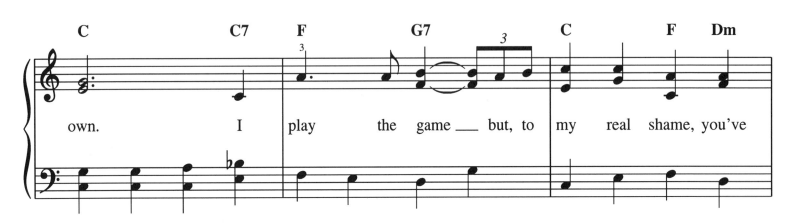

own. I play the game __ but, to my real shame, you've

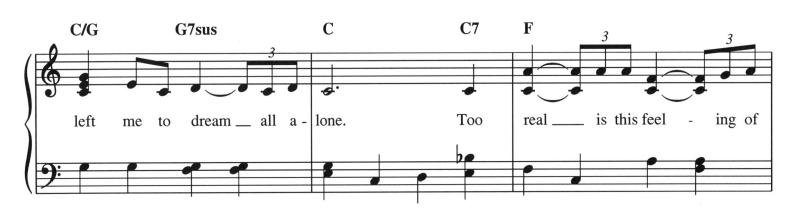

left me to dream __ all a - lone. Too real __ is this feel - ing of

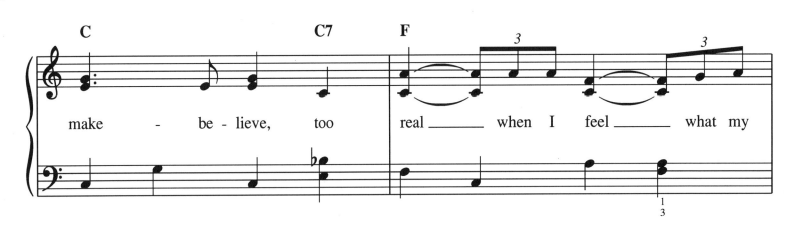

make - be - lieve, too real __ when I feel __ what my

heart __ can't con-ceal. Oh, ___ yes, __ I'm the great pre - tend - er, ___ just

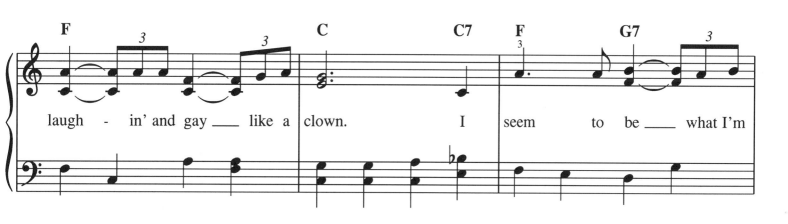

laugh - in' and gay ___ like a clown. I seem to be ___ what I'm

not, you see, I'm wear-in' my heart ___ like a crown; pre -

tend - in' that you're __ still a - roun'. Oh, roun'.

rit.

HAVE I TOLD YOU LATELY
THAT I LOVE YOU

Words and Music by
SCOTT WISEMAN

MCA music publishing

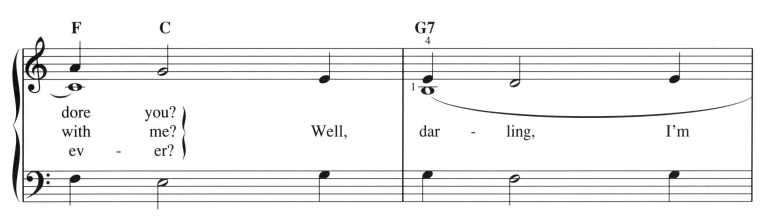

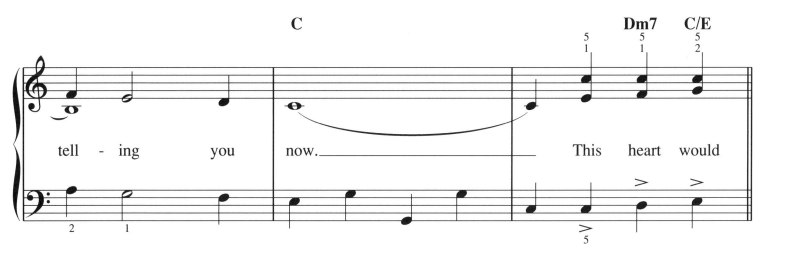

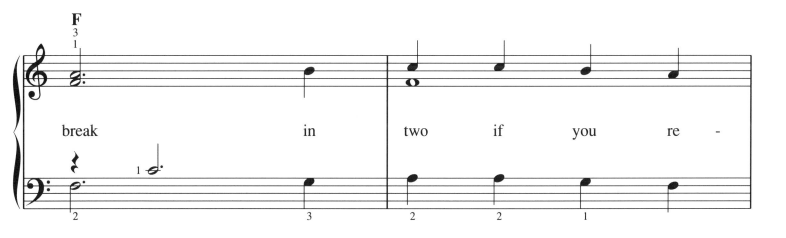

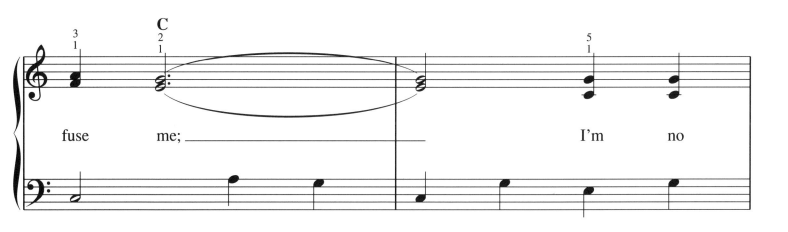

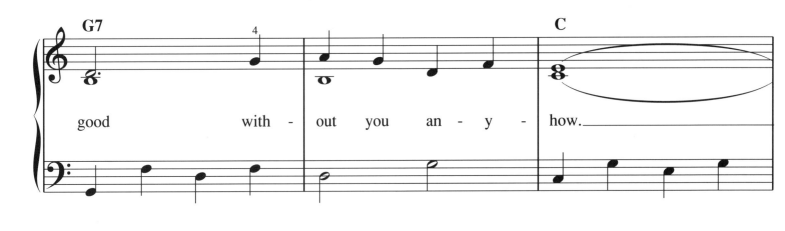

good with - out you an - y - how.

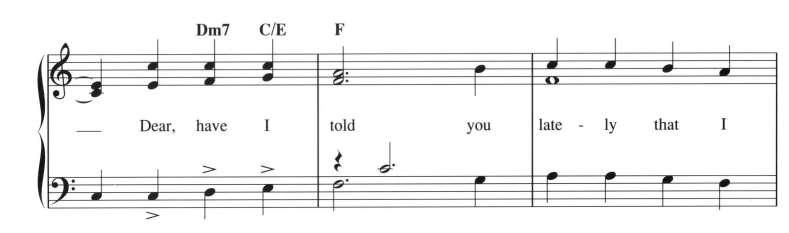

Dear, have I told you late - ly that I

love you? Well, dar - ling, I'm

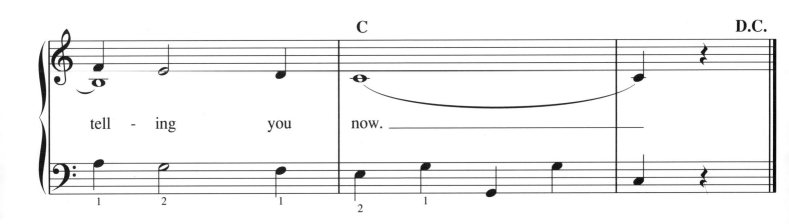

tell - ing you now.

I LOVE YOU
from MEXICAN HAYRIDE

Words and Music by
COLE PORTER

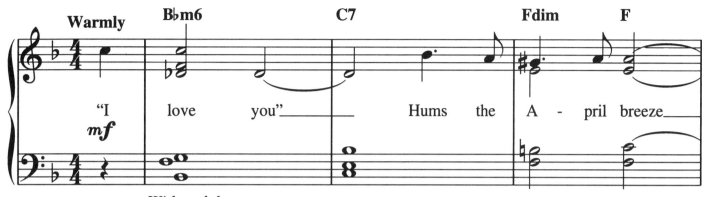

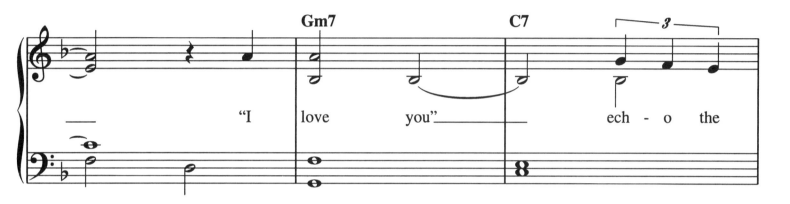

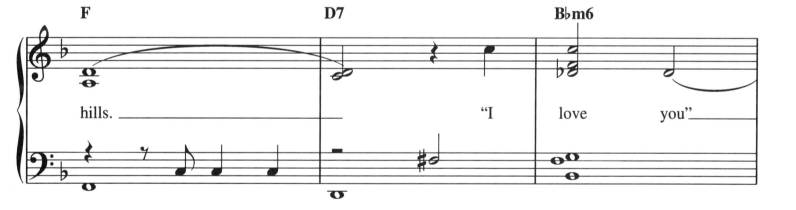

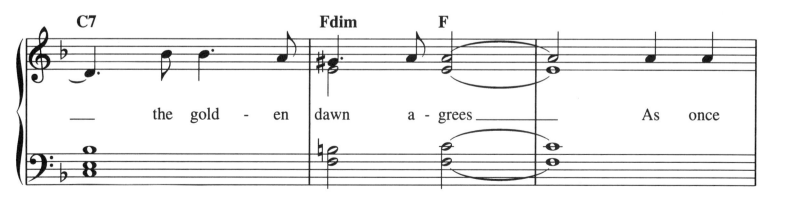

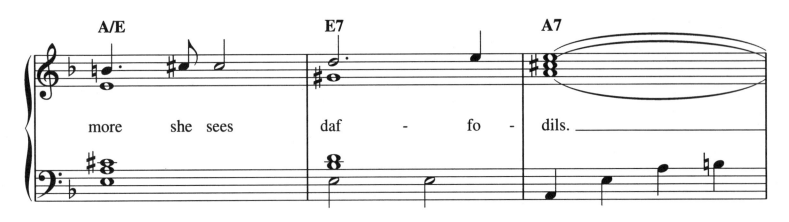

more she sees daf - fo - dils. _____

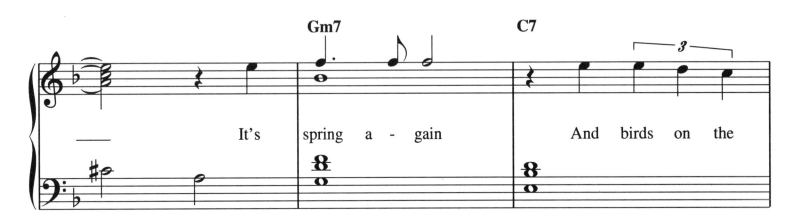

____ It's spring a - gain And birds on the

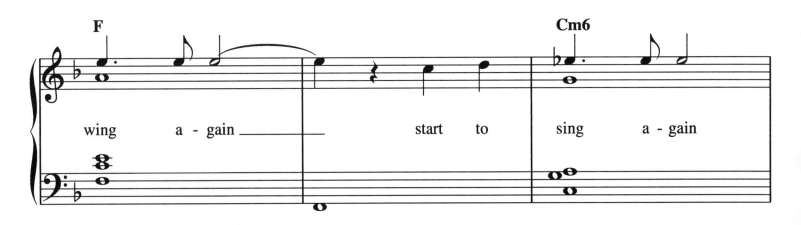

wing a - gain _____ start to sing a - gain

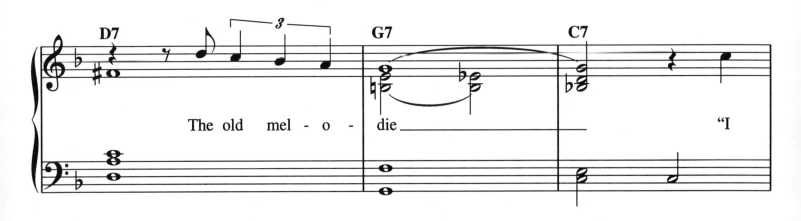

The old mel - o - die _____ "I

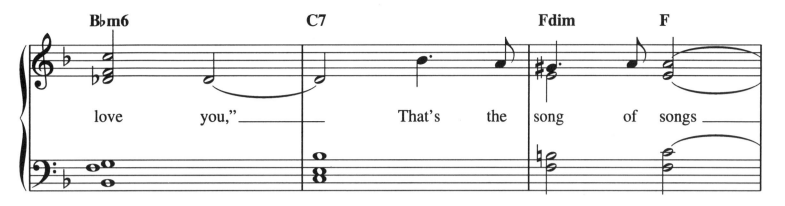

love you," _____ That's the song of songs _____

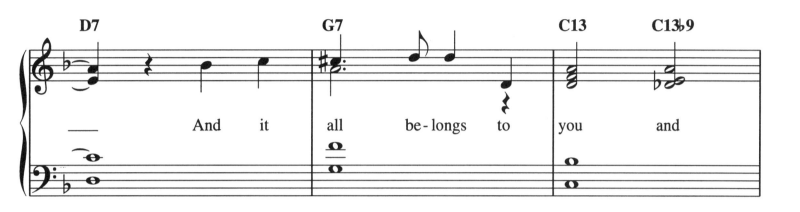

_____ And it all be-longs to you and

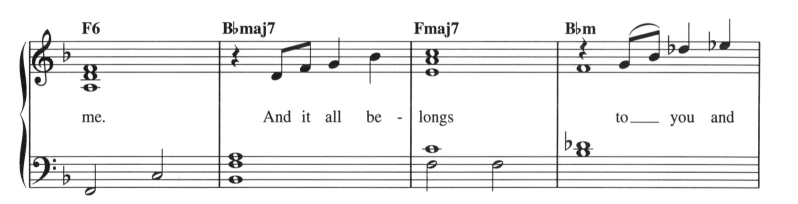

me. And it all be - longs to _____ you and

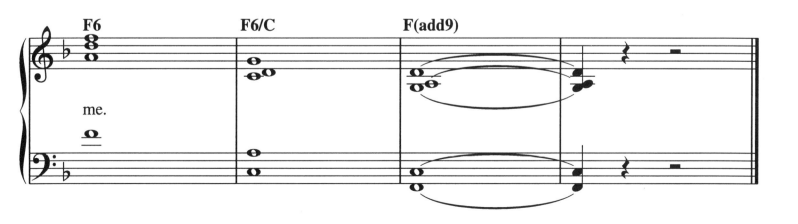

me.

HELLO, YOUNG LOVERS
from THE KING AND I

Lyrics by OSCAR HAMMERSTEIN II
Music by RICHARD RODGERS

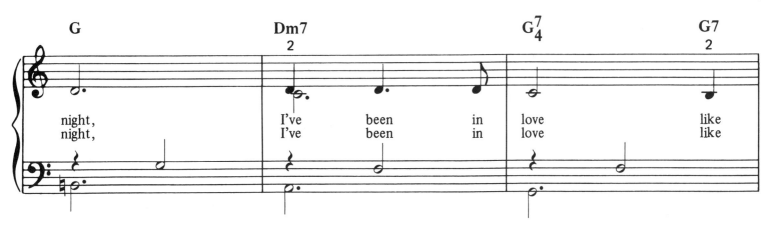

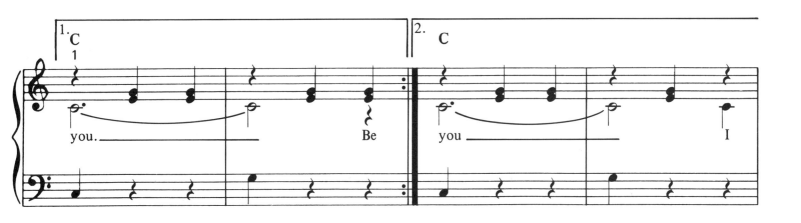

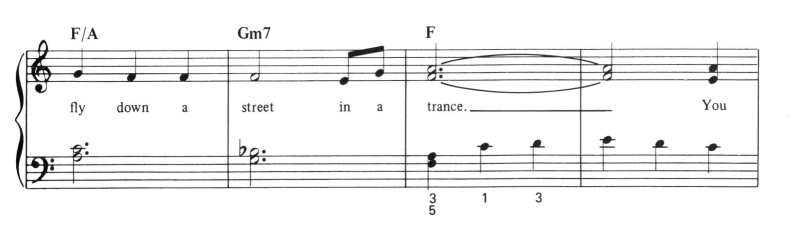

fly down a street on a chance that you'll meet, and you

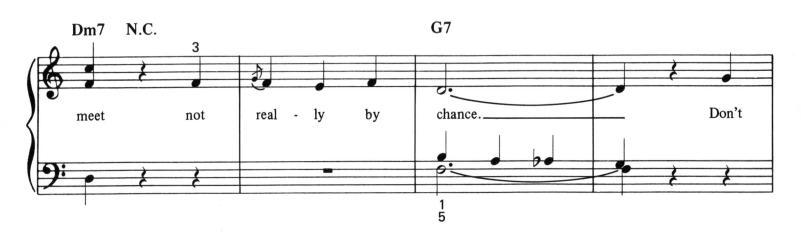

meet not real - ly by chance._____ Don't

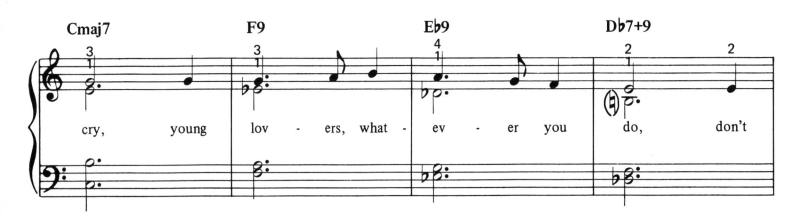

cry, young lov - ers, what - ev - er you do, don't

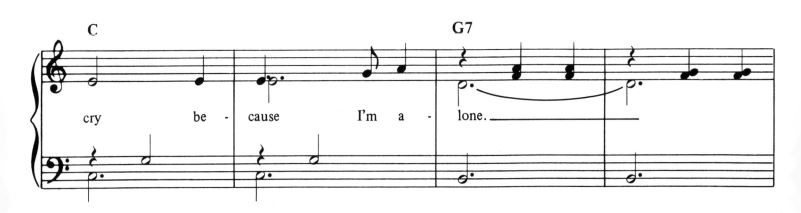

cry be - cause I'm a - lone._____

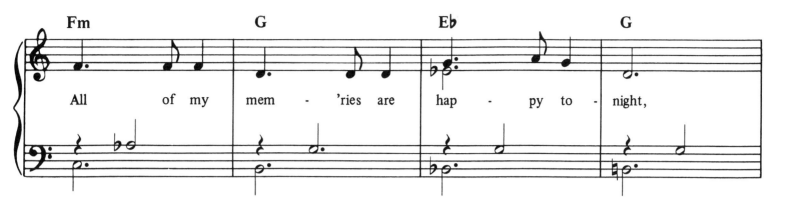

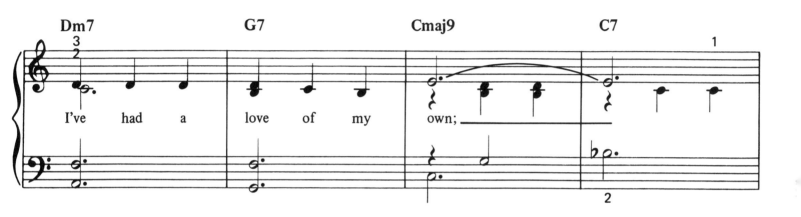

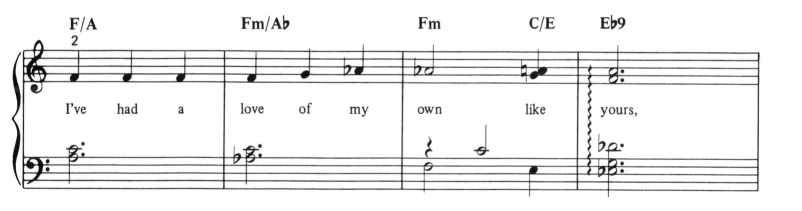

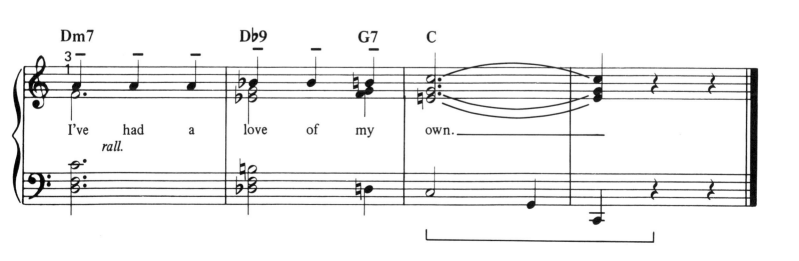

I COULD WRITE A BOOK

from PAL JOEY

Words by LORENZ HART
Music by RICHARD RODGERS

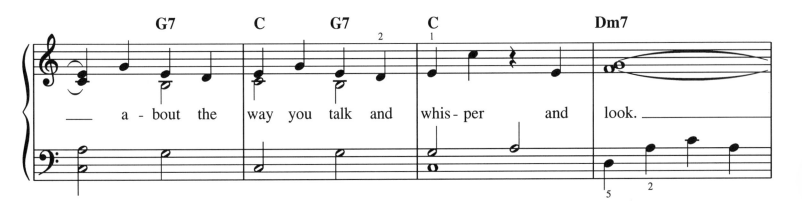

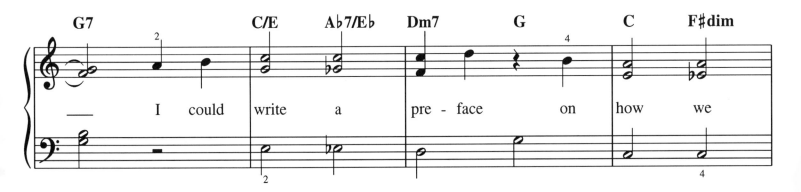

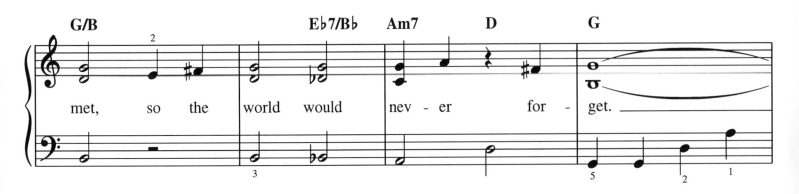

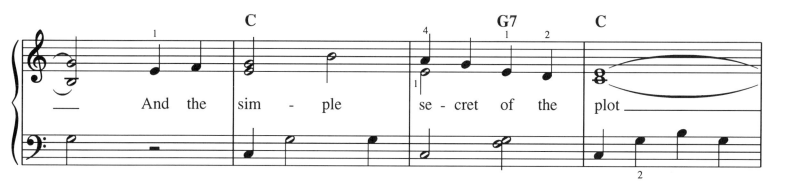

And the sim - ple se - cret of the plot ___

___ is just to tell them that I love you a lot. ___

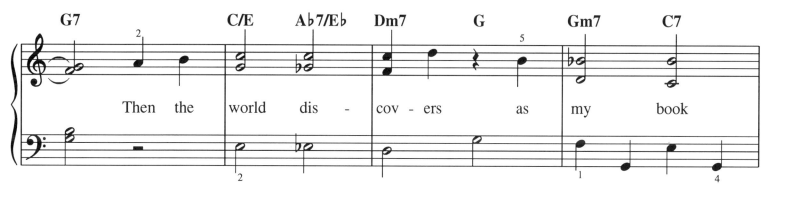

Then the world dis - cov - ers as my book

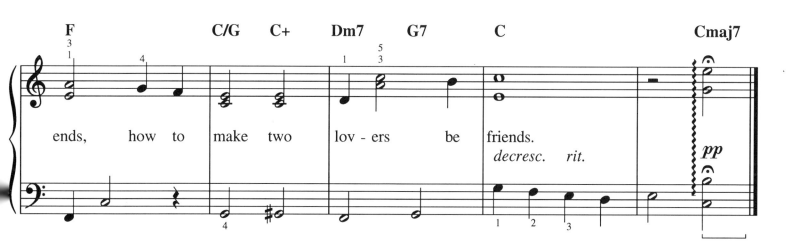

ends, how to make two lov - ers be friends.

decresc. rit.

pp

I HAVE DREAMED
from THE KING AND I

Lyrics by OSCAR HAMMERSTEIN II
Music by RICHARD RODGERS

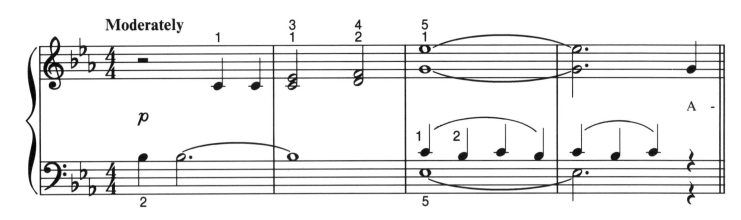

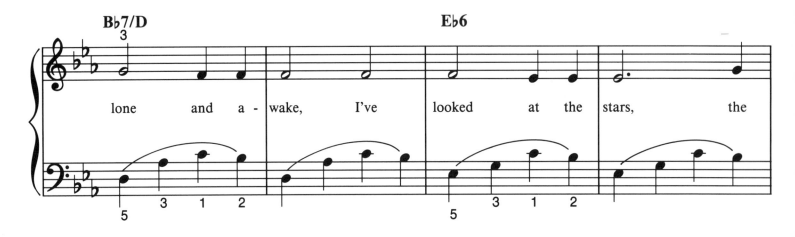

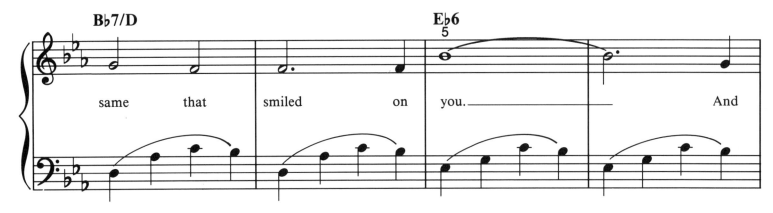

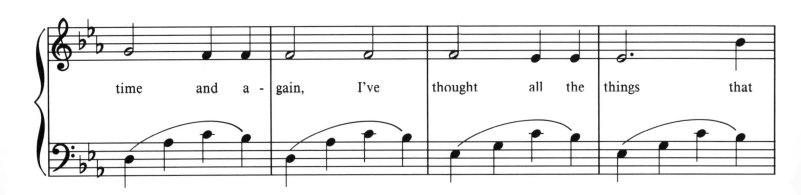

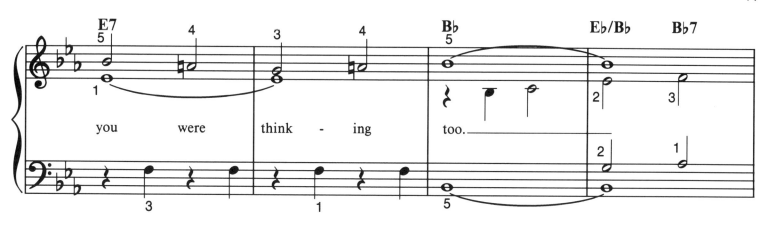

Slowly, very smoothly

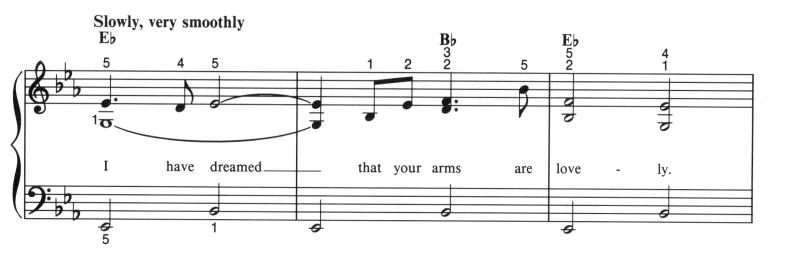

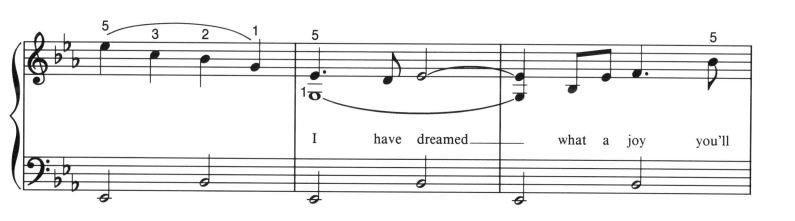

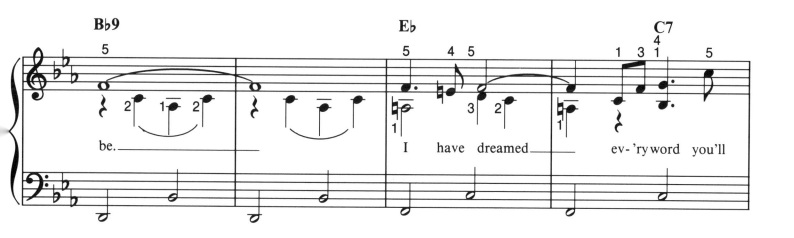

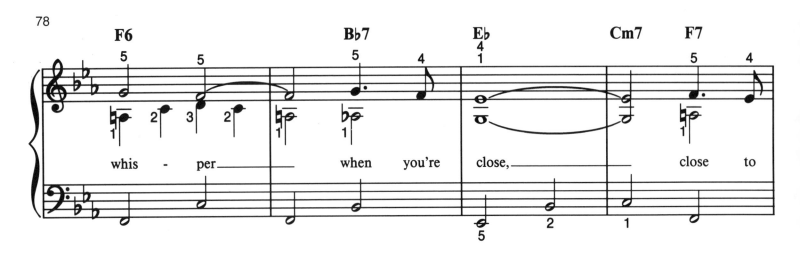

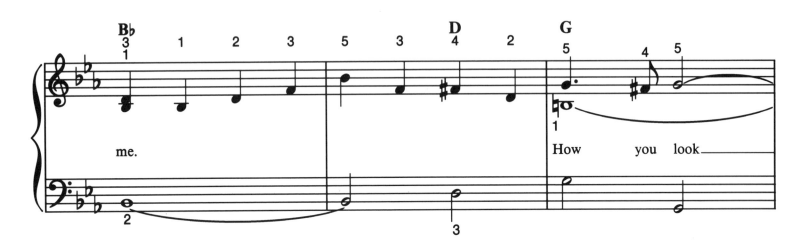

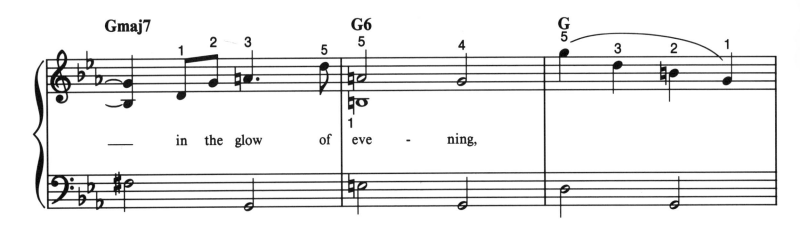

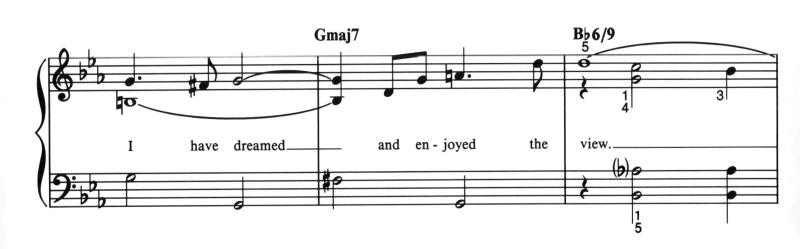

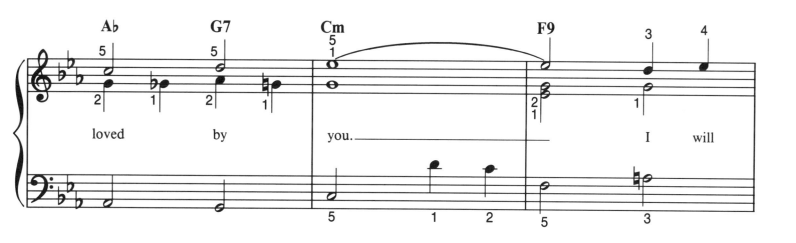

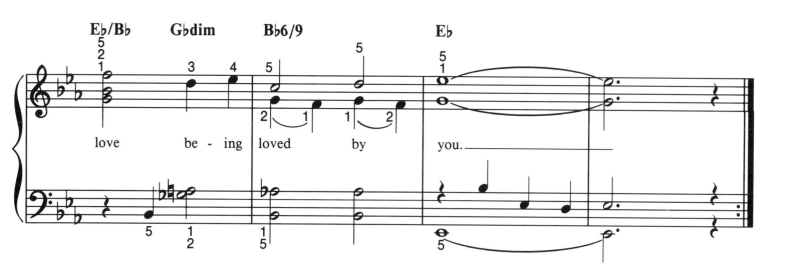

I'LL BE SEEING YOU
from RIGHT THIS WAY

Lyric by IRVING KAHAL
Music by SAMMY FAIN

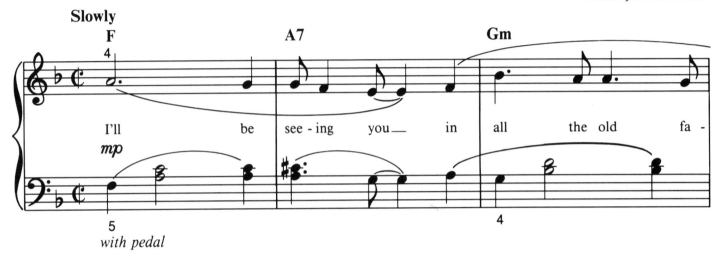

I'll be see-ing you___ in all the old fa-

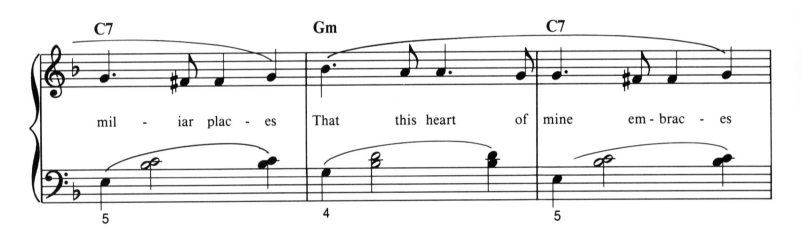

mil - iar plac - es That this heart of mine em-brac - es

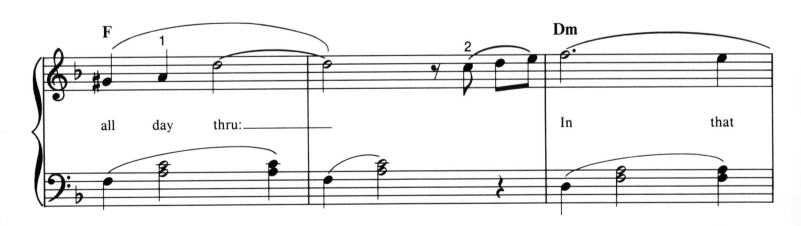

all day thru:___ In that

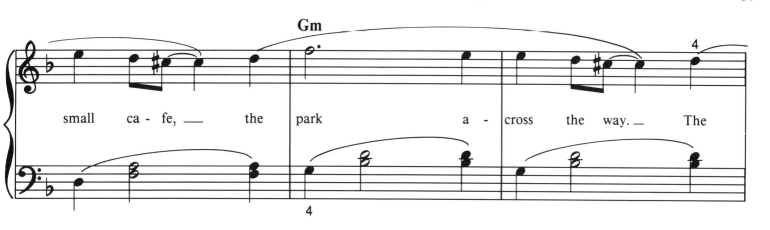

small ca - fe, ___ the park a - cross the way. ___ The

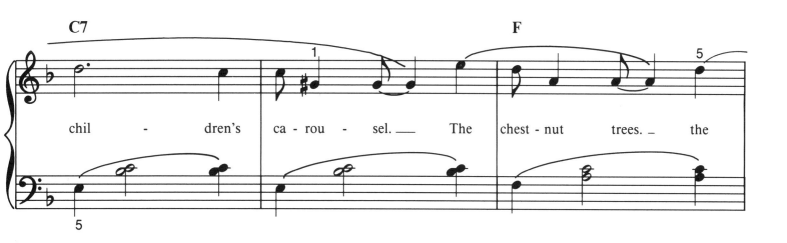

chil - dren's ca - rou - sel. ___ The chest - nut trees. ___ the

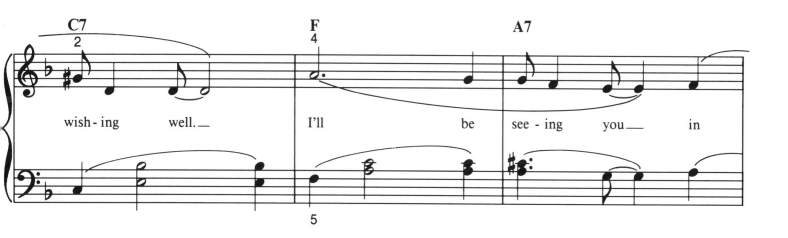

wish - ing well. ___ I'll be see - ing you ___ in

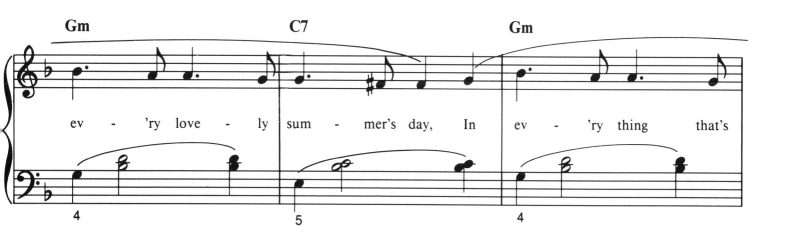

ev - 'ry love - ly sum - mer's day, In ev - 'ry thing that's

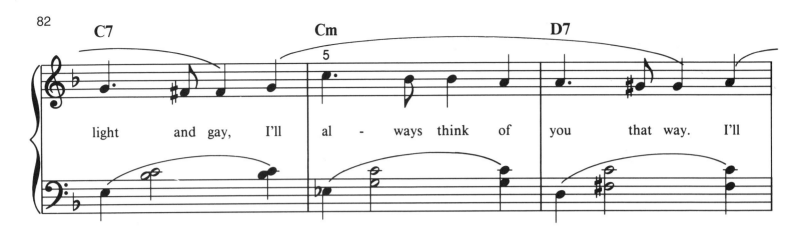

light   and   gay,   I'll   al - ways   think   of   you   that   way.   I'll

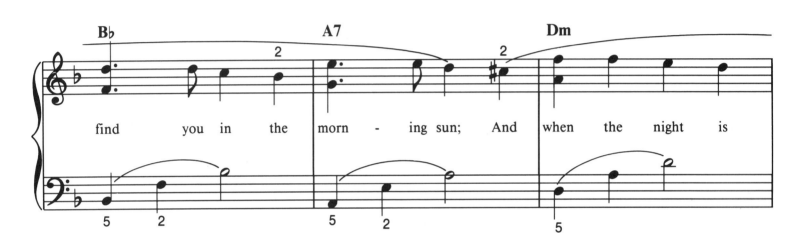

find   you   in   the   morn - ing   sun;   And   when   the   night   is

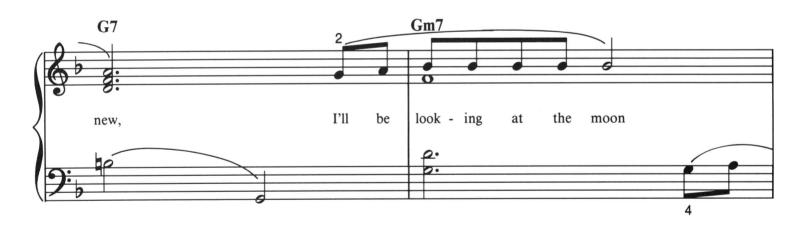

new,   I'll   be   look - ing   at   the   moon

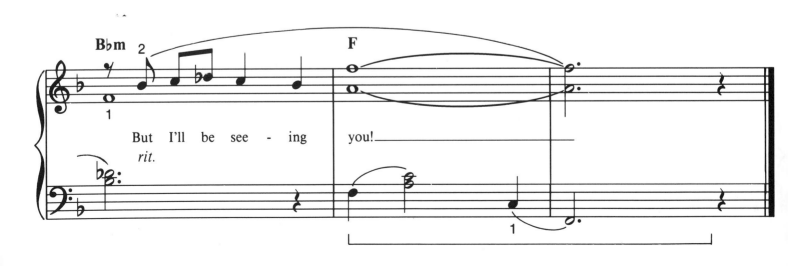

But   I'll   be   see - ing   you!

rit.

I'M BEGINNING TO SEE THE LIGHT

Words and Music by DON GEORGE, JOHNNY HODGES, DUKE ELLINGTON and HARRY JAMES

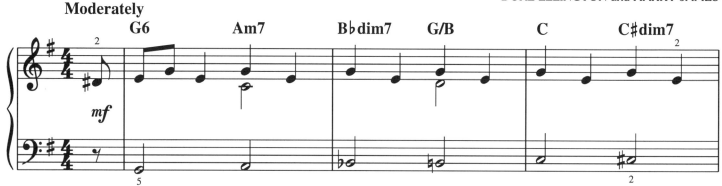

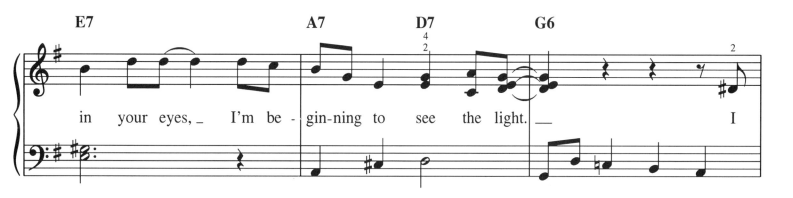

nev - er went in for af - ter glow, _ Or can - dle - light on the

mis - tle - toe, _ But now when you turn the lamp down low _ I'm be -

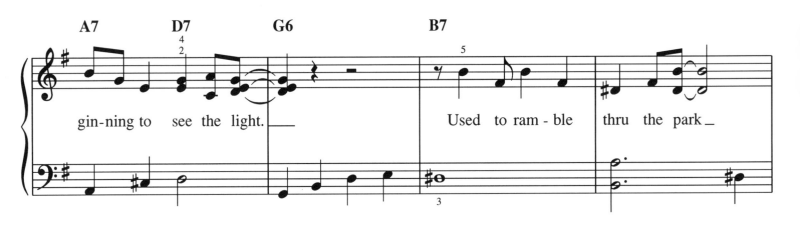

gin - ning to see the light. _ Used to ram - ble thru the park _

Shad - ow box - ing in the dark _ Then you came and

caused a spark, _ That's a four a-larm fire _____ now. I

nev-er made love by lan-tern shine, _ I nev-er saw rain-bows

in my wine, _ But now that your lips are burn-ing mine, _ I'm be-

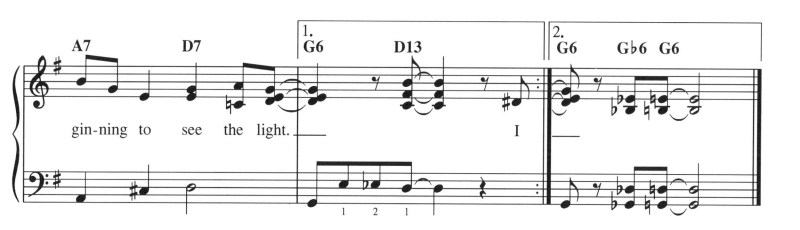

gin-ning to see the light. ___ I

I'VE GROWN ACCUSTOMED TO HER FACE

from MY FAIR LADY

Words by ALAN JAY LERNER
Music by FREDERICK LOEWE

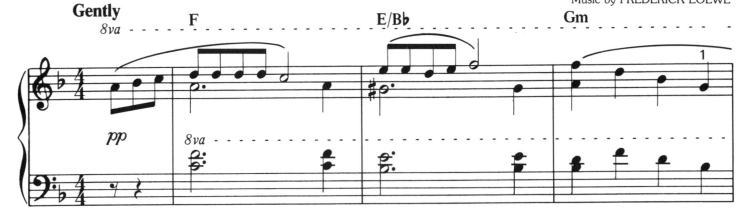

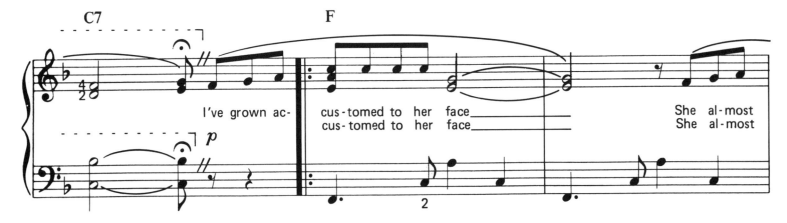

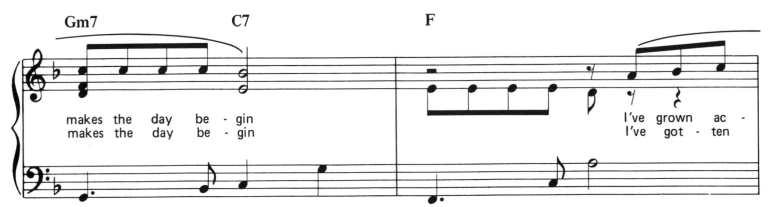

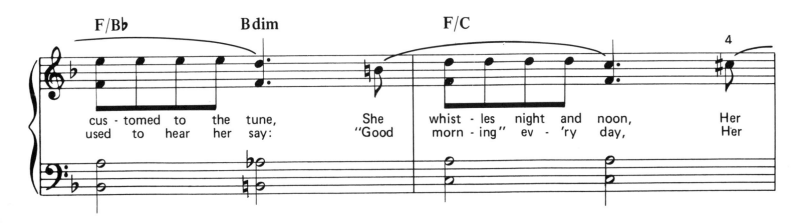

87

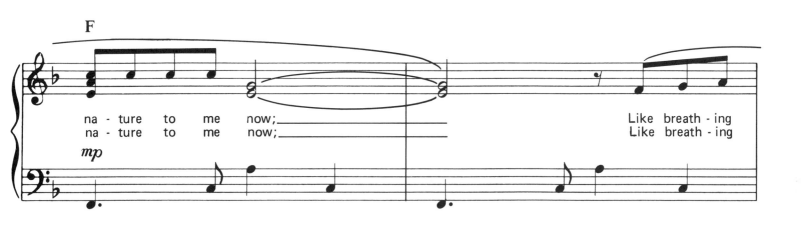

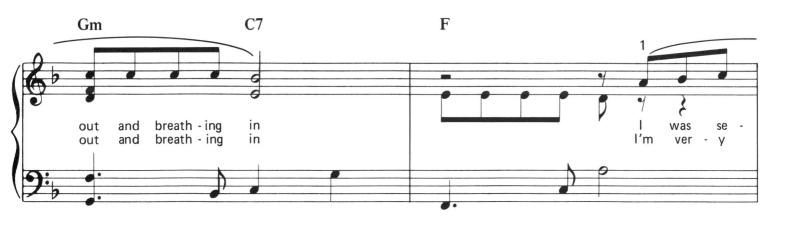

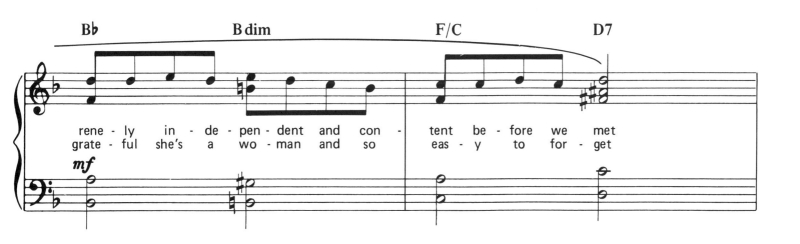

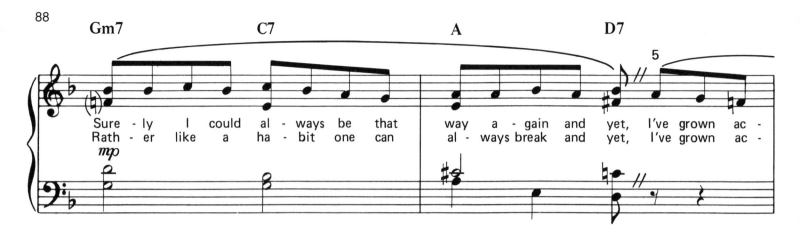

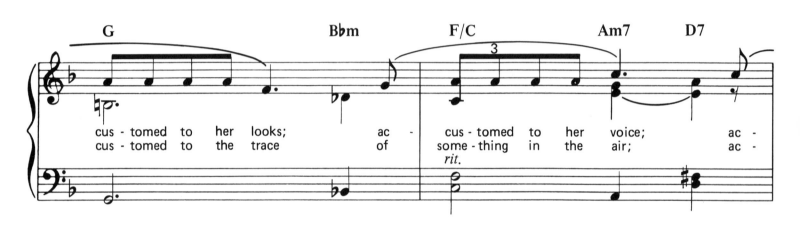

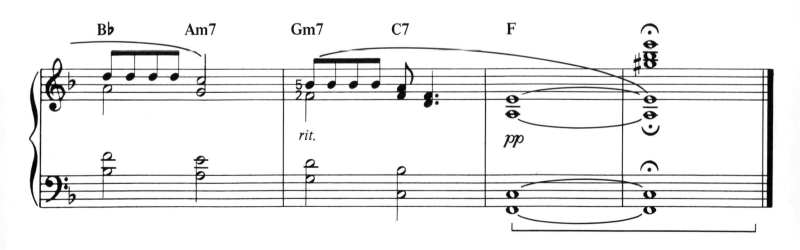

IF I LOVED YOU
from CAROUSEL

Lyrics by OSCAR HAMMERSTEIN II
Music by RICHARD RODGERS

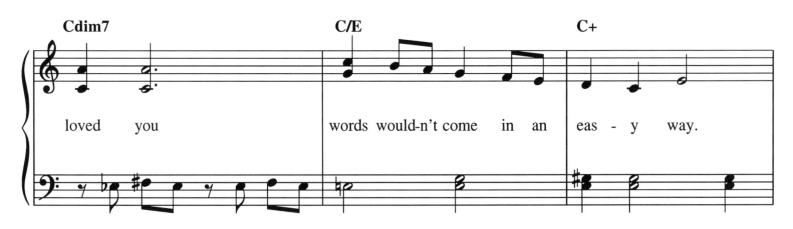

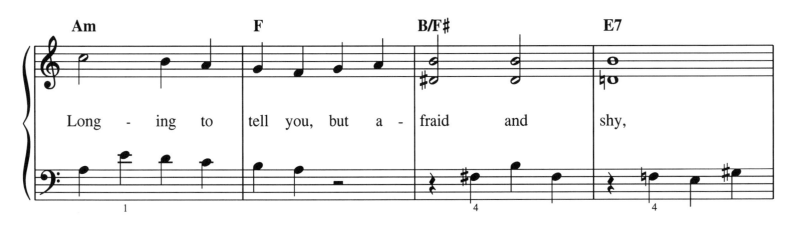

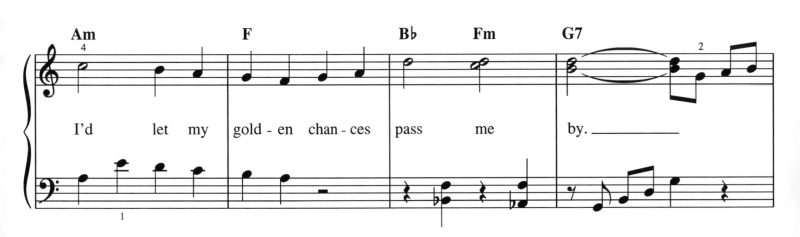

IN THE WEE SMALL HOURS
OF THE MORNING

Words by BOB HILLIARD
Music by DAVID MANN

93

JUST IN TIME
from BELLS ARE RINGING

Words by BETTY COMDEN and ADOLPH GREEN
Music by JULE STYNE

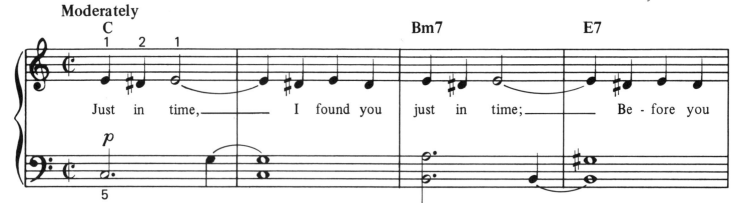

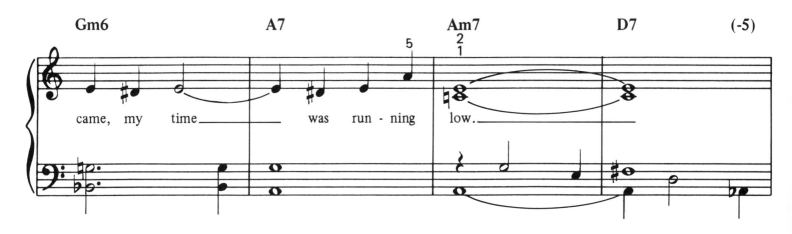

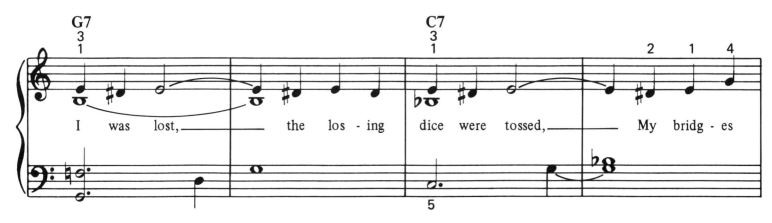

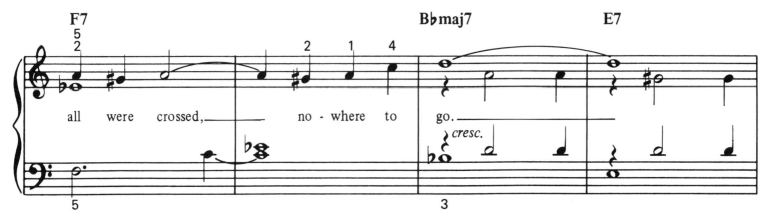

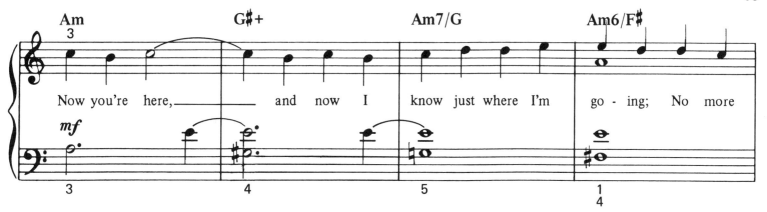

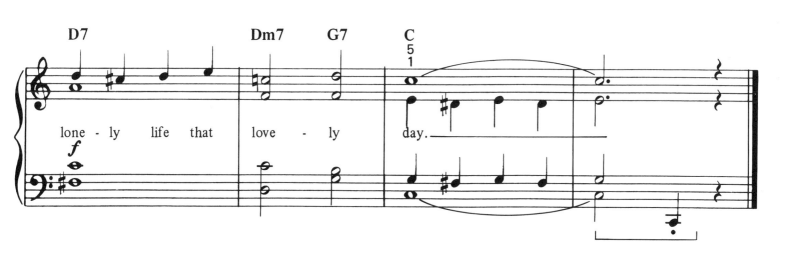

LA VIE EN ROSE

Original French Words by EDITH PIAF
English Words by MACK DAVID
Music by LOUIGUY

Freely

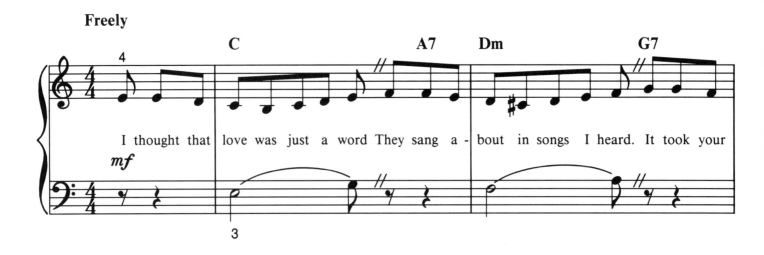

I thought that love was just a word They sang a - bout in songs I heard. It took your

kiss - es to re - veal That I was wrong and love is real.

Chorus
Slowly, with expression

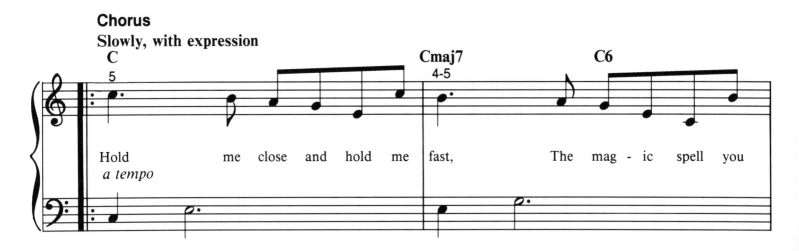

Hold me close and hold me fast, The mag - ic spell you

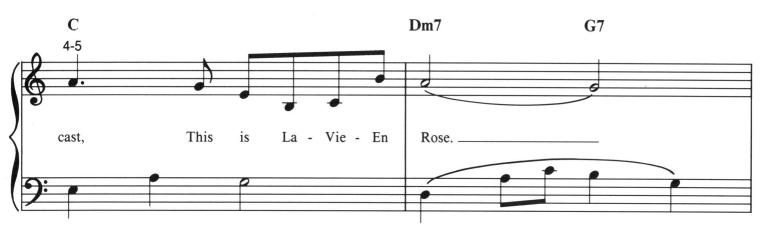

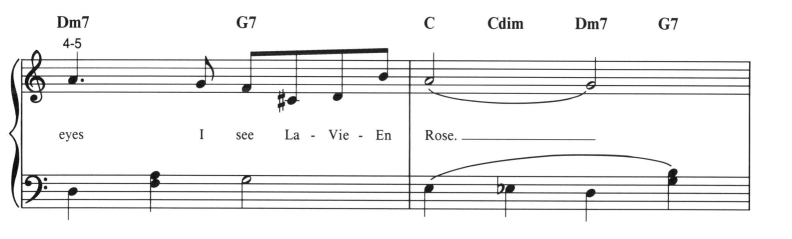

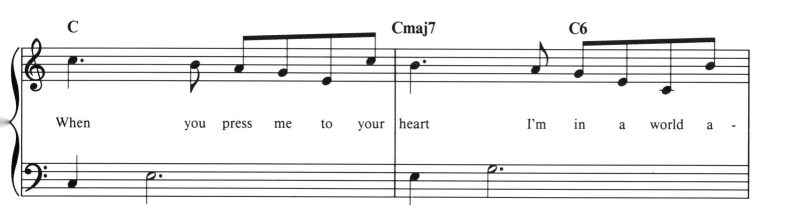

part, A world where ros - es bloom; And when you speak An - gels

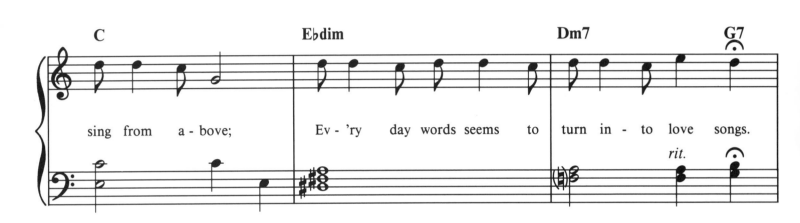

sing from a - bove; Ev - 'ry day words seems to turn in - to love songs.

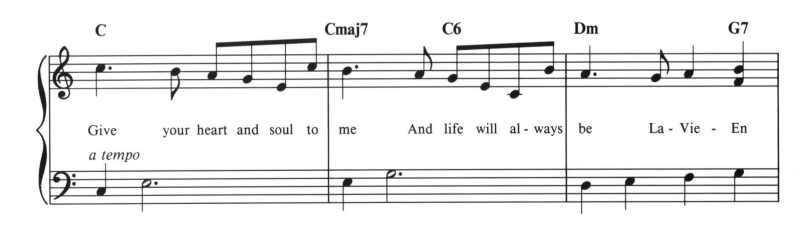

Give your heart and soul to me And life will al - ways be La - Vie - En

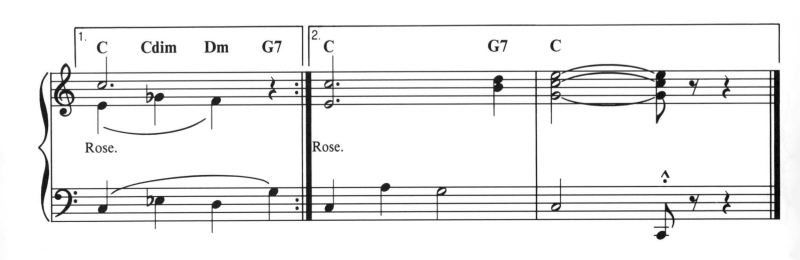

Rose. Rose.

LONG AGO
(And Far Away)
from COVER GIRL

Words by IRA GERSHWIN
Music by JEROME KERN

Long a - go and far a - way, I dreamed a dream one day, and now that dream is here be - side me. Long the

LOVE LETTERS
Theme from the Paramount Picture LOVE LETTERS

Words by EDWARD HEYMAN
Music by VICTOR YOUNG

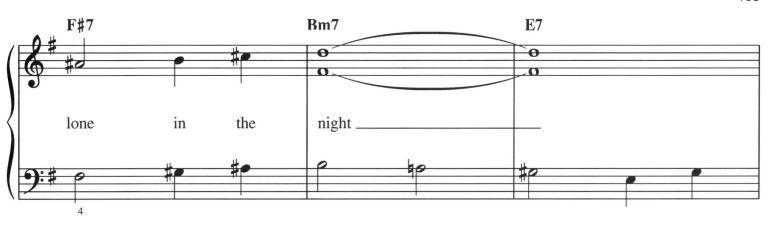

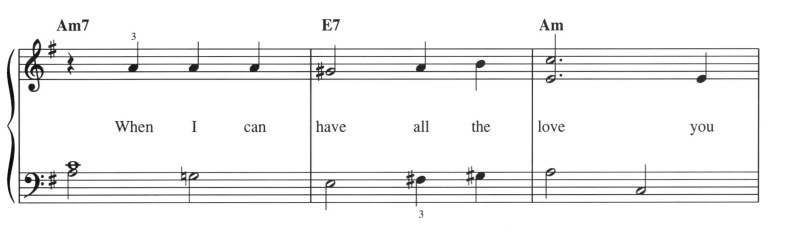

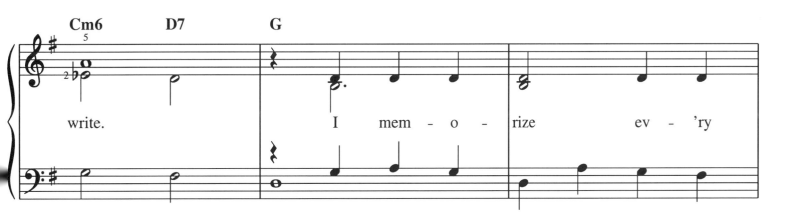

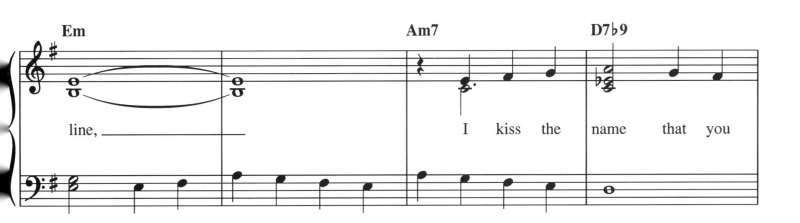

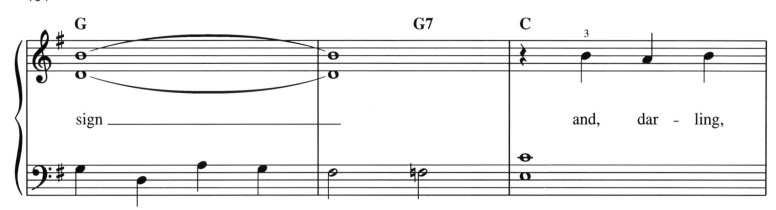

sign _____ and, dar - ling,

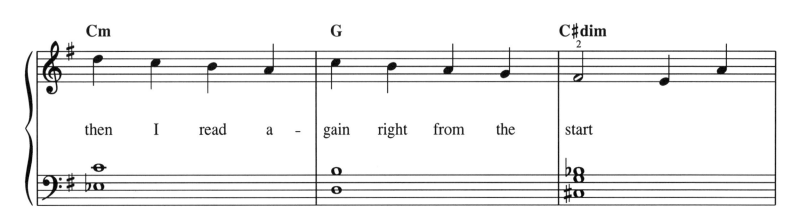

then I read a - gain right from the start

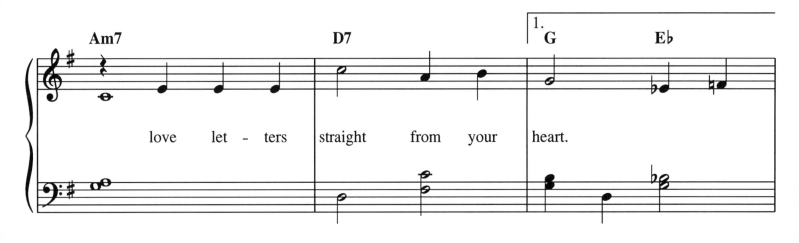

love let - ters straight from your heart.

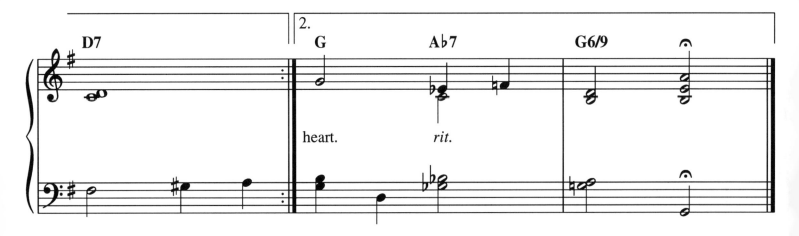

heart. *rit.*

MAGIC MOMENTS

Lyric by HAL DAVID
Music by BURT BACHARACH

Slow Shuffle

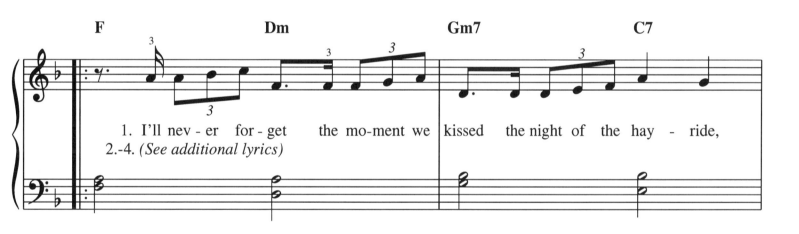

1. I'll nev-er for-get the mo-ment we kissed the night of the hay-ride,
2.-4. *(See additional lyrics)*

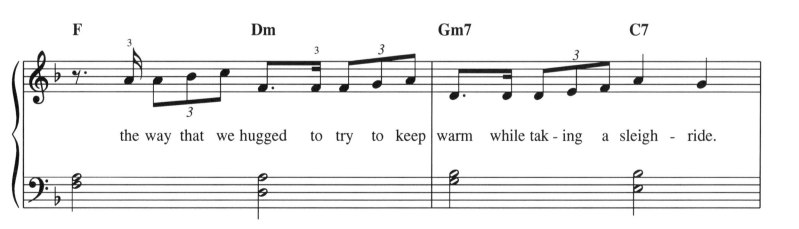

the way that we hugged to try to keep warm while tak-ing a sleigh-ride.

Chorus

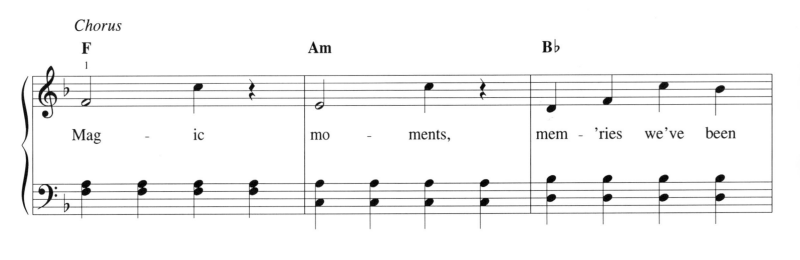

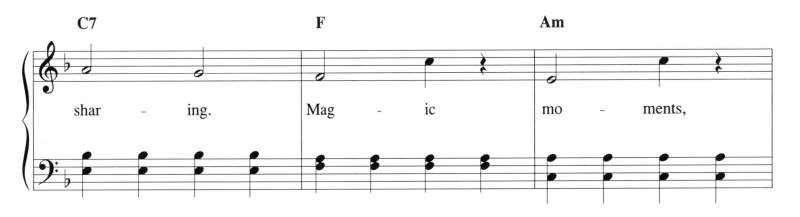

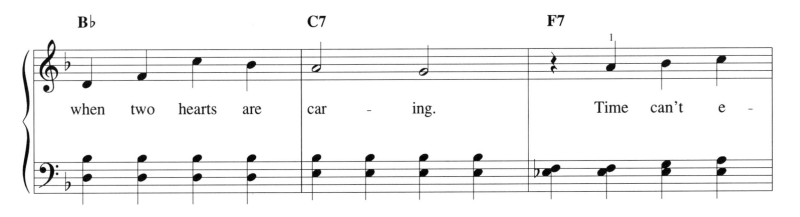

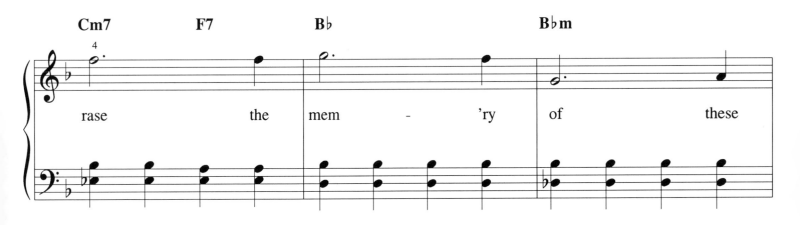

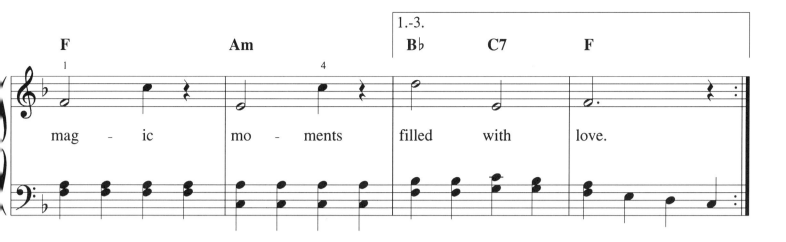

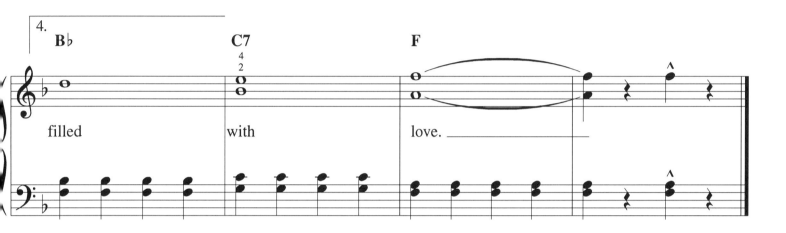

Additional Lyrics

2. The telephone call that tied up the line for hours and hours,
The Saturday dance { I / you } got up the nerve to send { you / me } some flowers.
To Chorus

3. The way that we cheered whenever our team was scoring a touchdown,
The time that the floor fell out of { my / your } car when { I / you } put the clutch down.
To Chorus

4. The penny arcade, the games that we played, the fun and the prizes,
The Halloween Hop when everyone came in funny disguises.
To Chorus

LOVE ME TENDER

Words and Music by ELVIS PRESLEY
and VERA MATSON

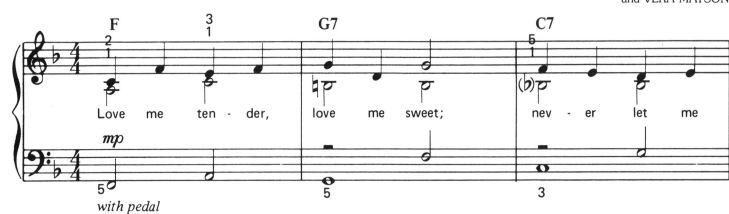

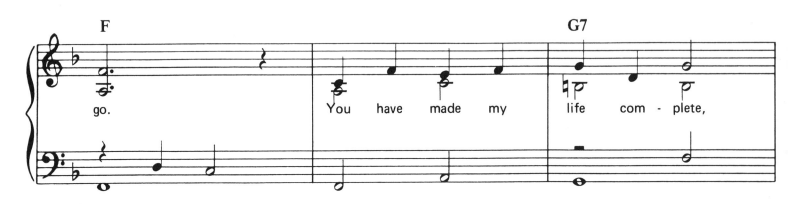

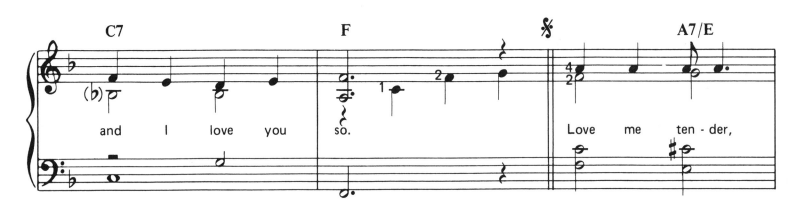

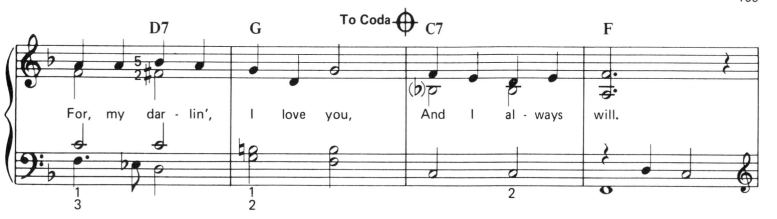

For, my dar-lin', I love you, And I al-ways will.

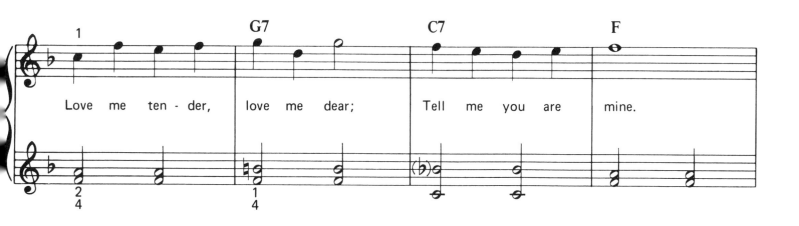

Love me ten-der, love me dear; Tell me you are mine.

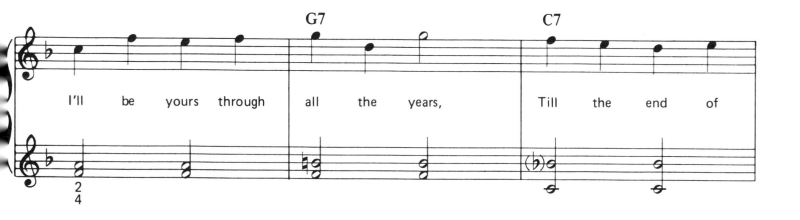

I'll be yours through all the years, Till the end of

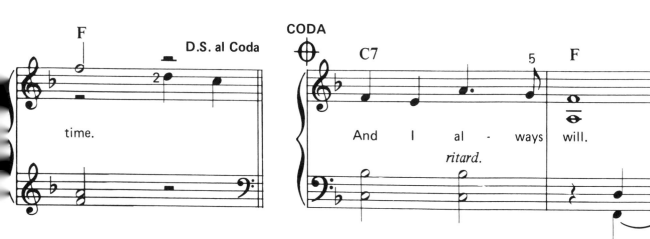

time. And I al-ways will.

MARIA ELENA

English Lyrics by S.K. RUSSELL
Music and Spanish Lyrics by LORENZO BARCELATA

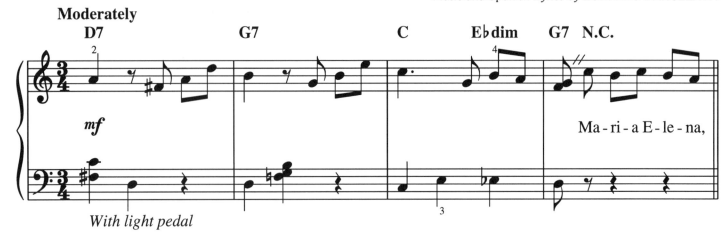

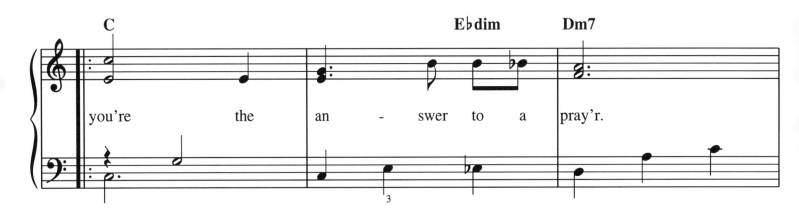

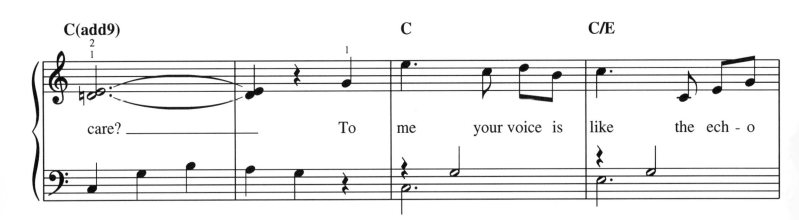

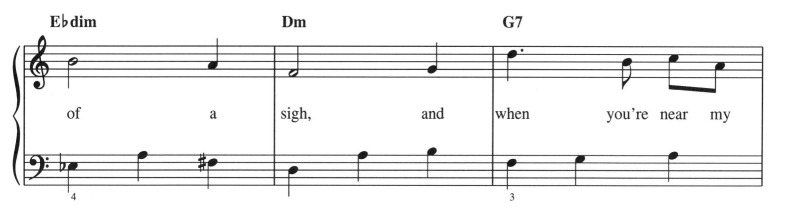

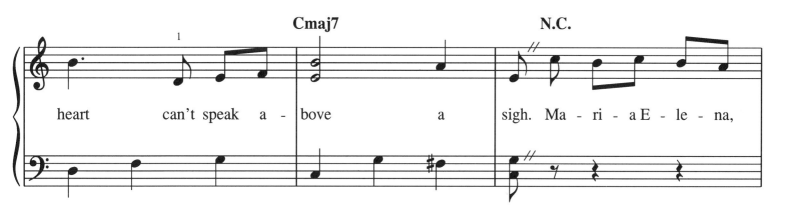

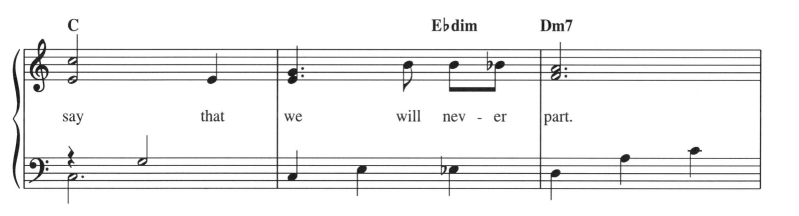

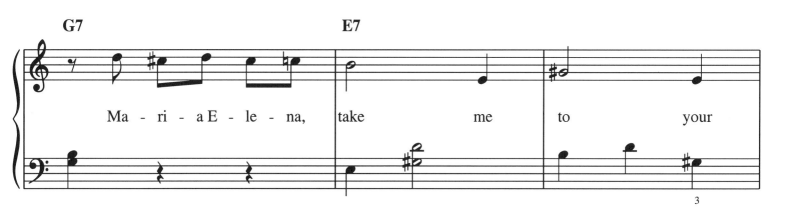

112

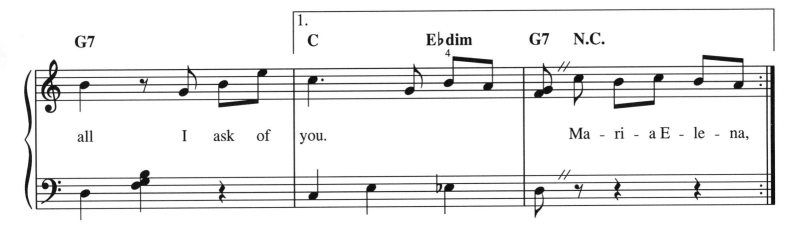

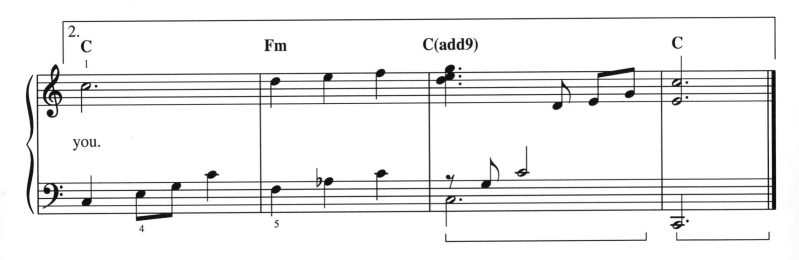

MEMORIES ARE MADE OF THIS

Words and Music by RICHARD DEHR,
FRANK MILLER and TERRY GILKYSON

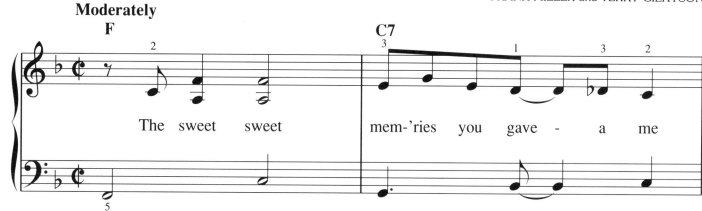

The sweet sweet mem-'ries you gave - a me

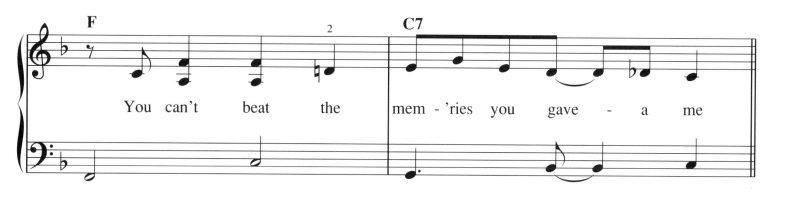

You can't beat the mem - 'ries you gave - a me

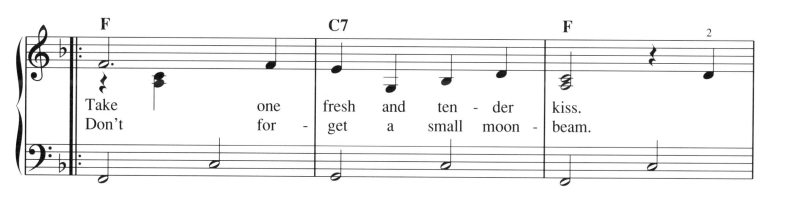

Take one fresh and ten - der kiss.
Don't for - get a small moon - beam.

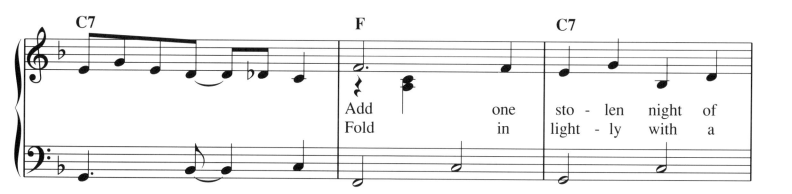

Add one sto - len night of
Fold in light - ly with a

bliss.
dream.

One girl,
Your lips

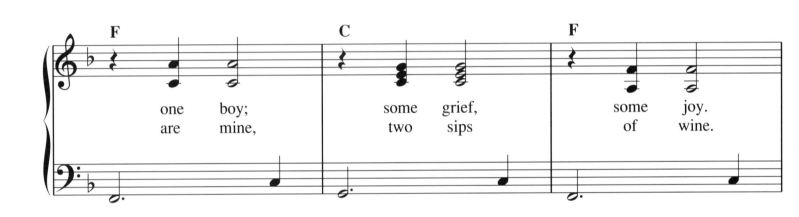

one boy;
are mine,

some grief,
two sips

some joy.
of wine.

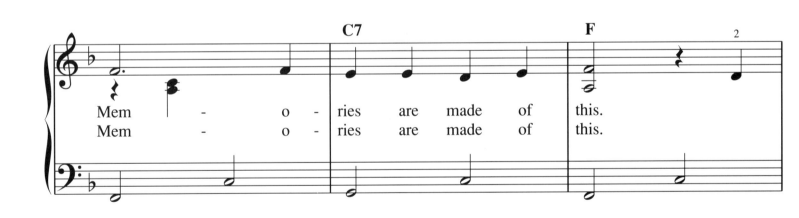

Mem - o - ries are made of this.
Mem - o - ries are made of this.

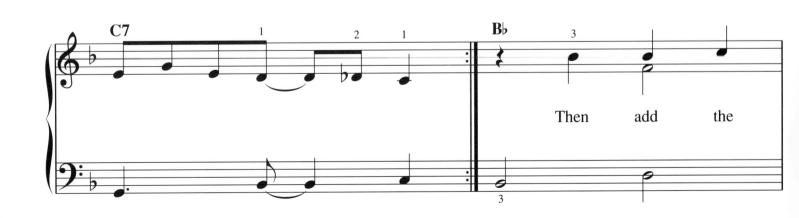

Then add the

wed - ding bells, _ one house where lov - ers dwell _

Three lit - tle kids for the fla - vor.

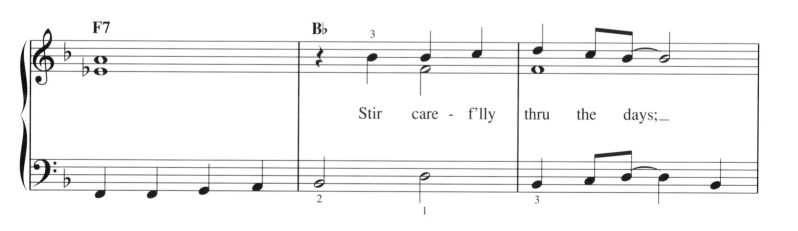

Stir care - f'lly thru the days; _

See how the fla - vor stays _ These are the

116

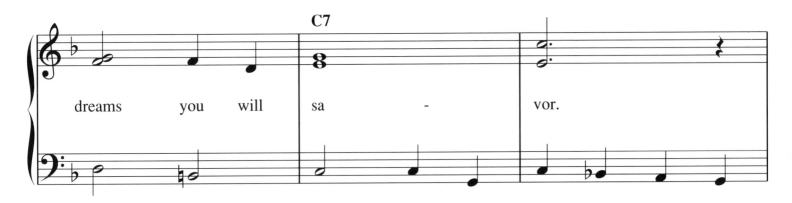

dreams   you   will   sa   -   vor.

With   His   bless - ings   from   a - bove,

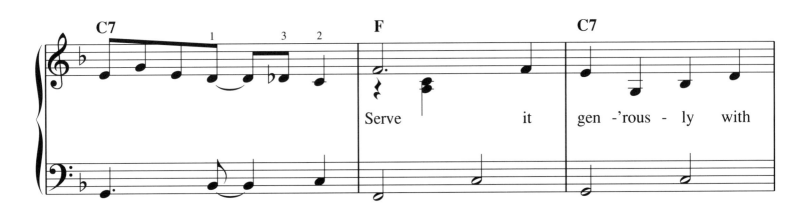

Serve   it   gen -'rous - ly   with

love.   One   man,

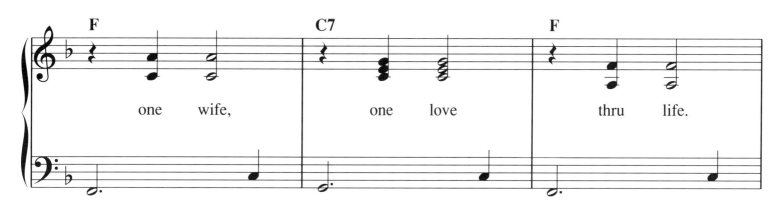

one wife, one love thru life.

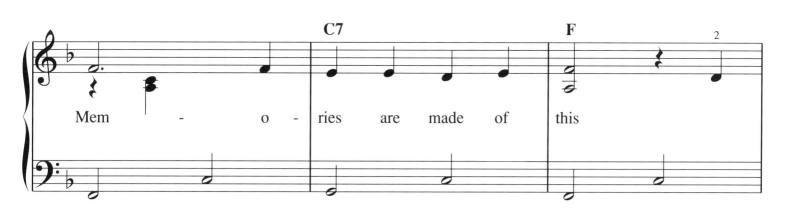

Mem - o - ries are made of this

Mem - o

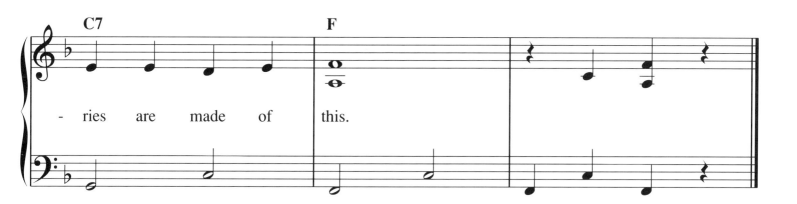

- ries are made of this.

MISTY

Words by JOHNNY BURKE
Music by ERROLL GARNER

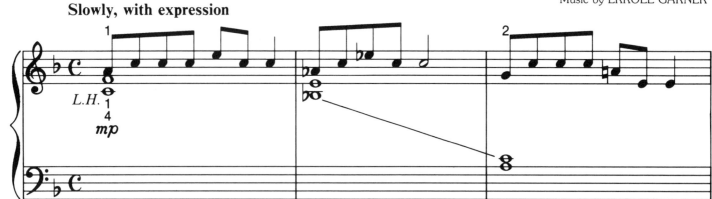

Look at me, I'm as help-less as a kit-ten up a

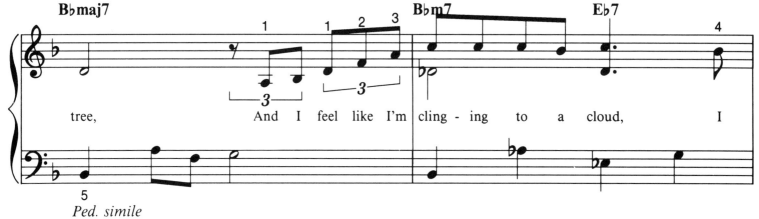

tree, And I feel like I'm cling-ing to a cloud, I

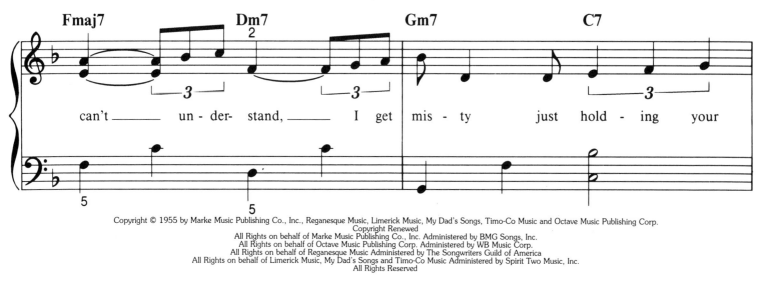

can't __ un-der-stand, __ I get mis-ty just hold-ing your

119

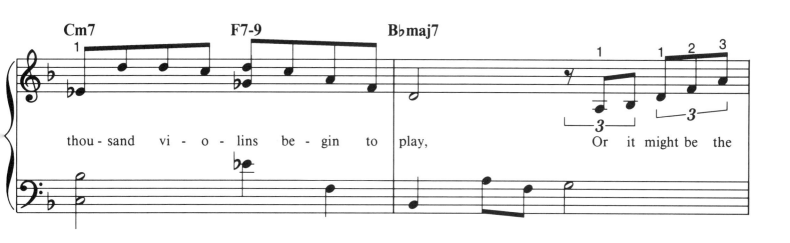

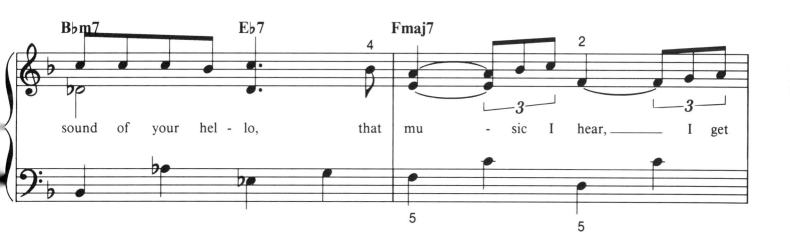

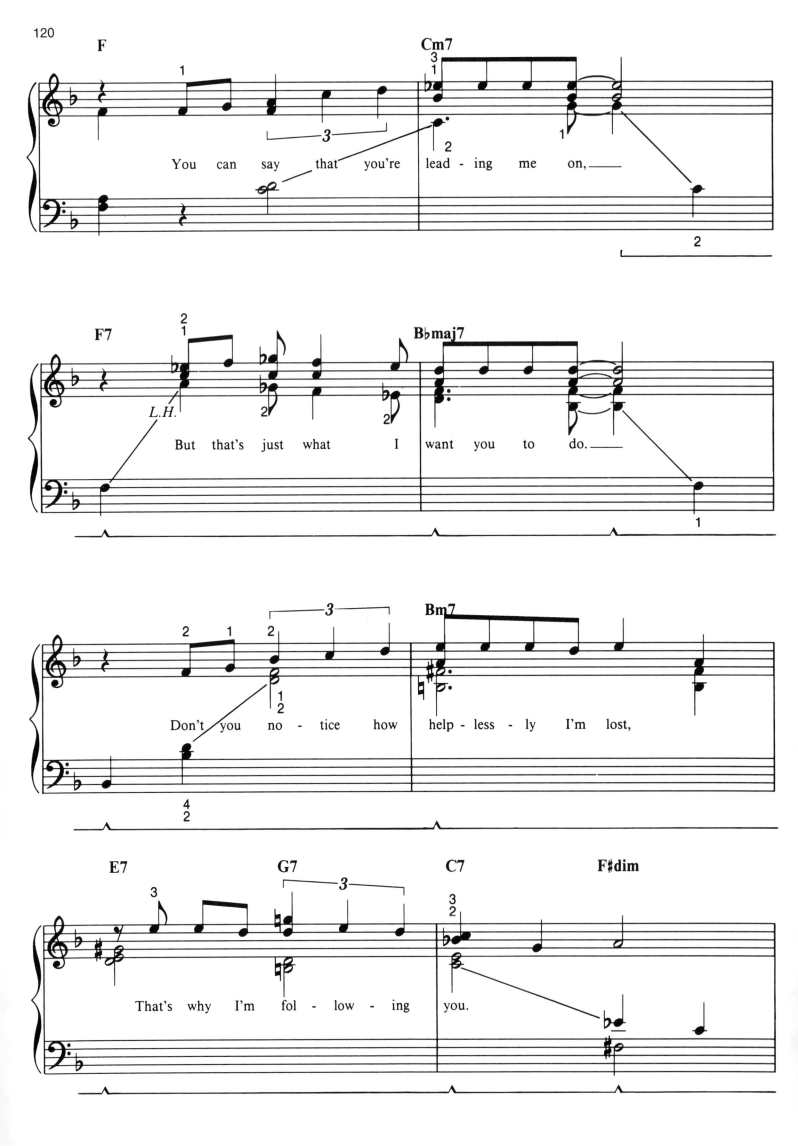

F

You can say that you're lead-ing me on, ___

Cm7

F7

But that's just what I want you to do. ___

B♭maj7

L.H.

Don't you no - tice how help - less - ly I'm lost,

Bm7

E7

That's why I'm fol - low - ing you.

G7

C7

F♯dim

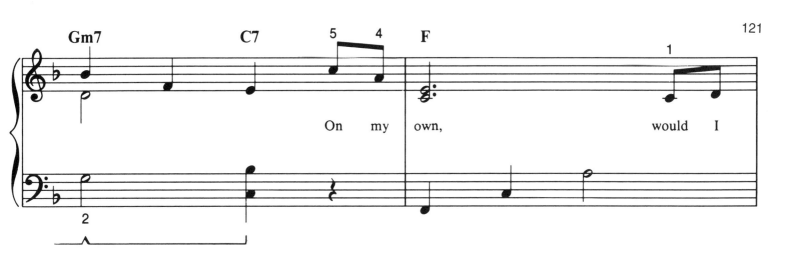

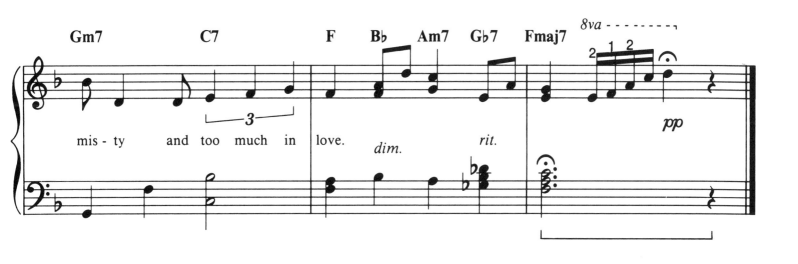

MOONLIGHT BECOMES YOU

from the Paramount Picture ROAD TO MOROCCO

Words by JOHNNY BURKE
Music by JAMES VAN HEUSEN

123

124

MY FOOLISH HEART

Words by NED WASHINGTON
Music by VICTOR YOUNG

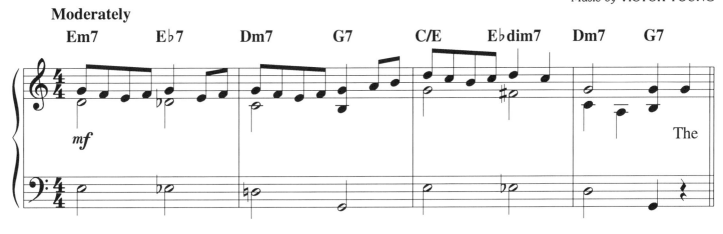

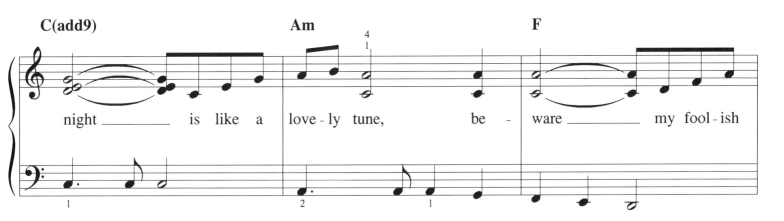

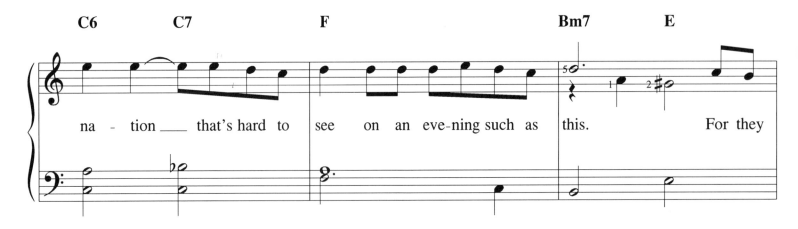

na - tion ____ that's hard to see on an eve-ning such as this. For they

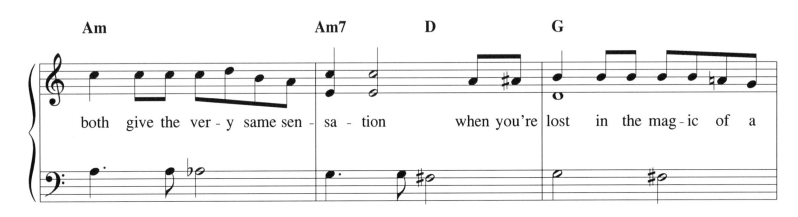

both give the ver - y same sen - sa - tion when you're lost in the mag - ic of a

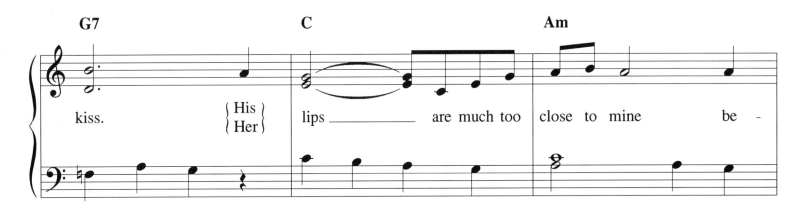

kiss. {His / Her} lips _____ are much too close to mine be -

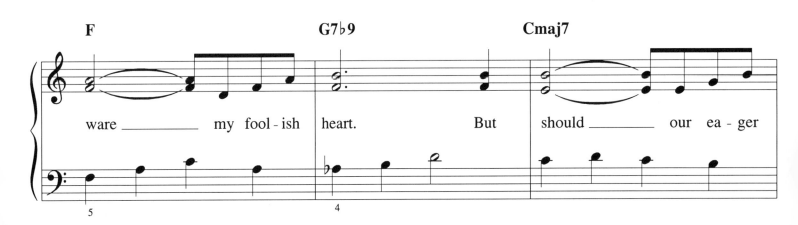

ware _____ my fool - ish heart. But should _____ our ea - ger

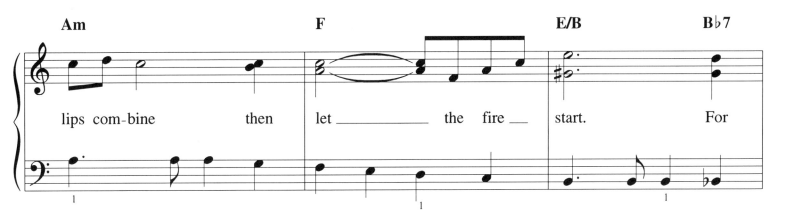

lips com-bine   then   let _____ the fire __ start.   For

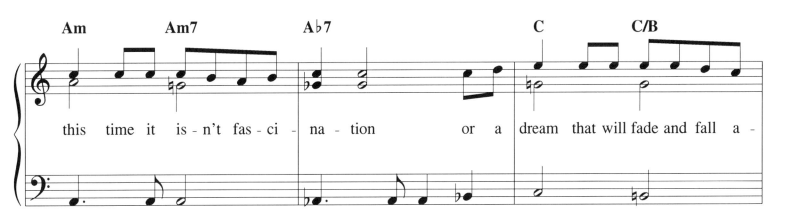

this time it is - n't fas-ci - na - tion   or a dream that will fade and fall a -

part.   It's love this time, it's love my fool - ish

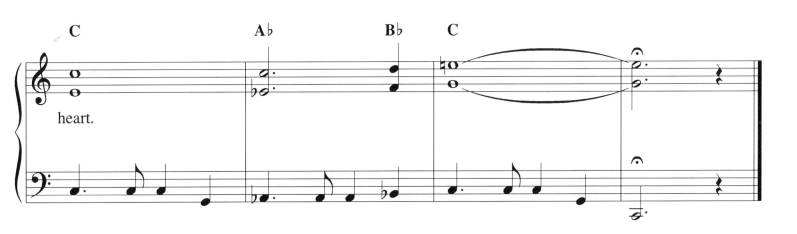

heart.

THE NEARNESS OF YOU
from the Paramount Picture ROMANCE IN THE DARK

Words by NED WASHINGTON
Music by HOAGY CARMICHAEL

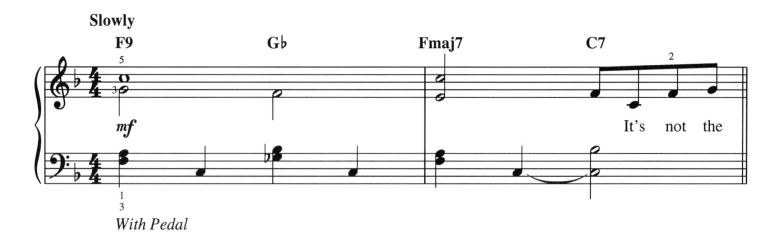

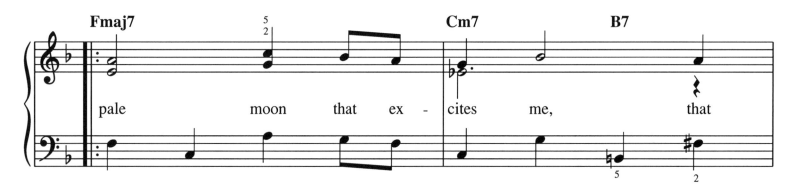

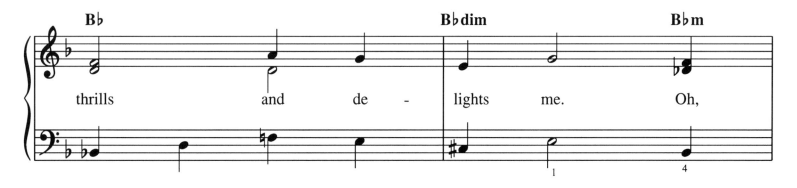

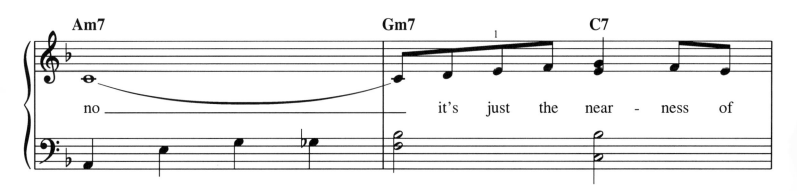

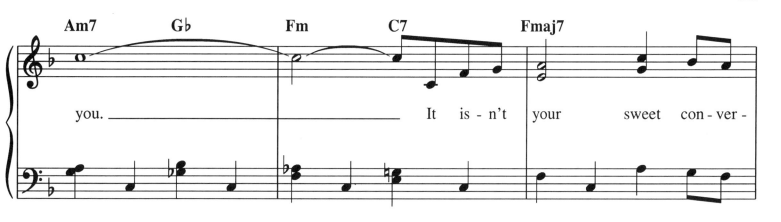

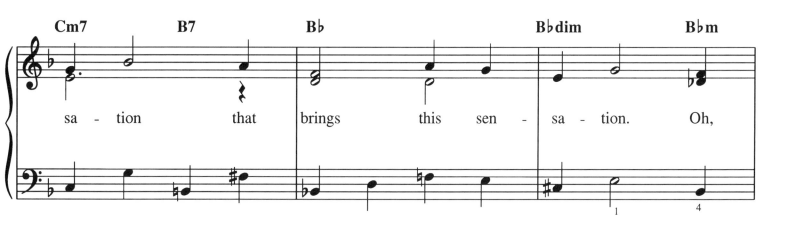

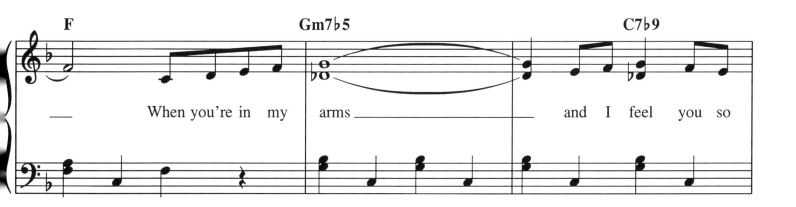

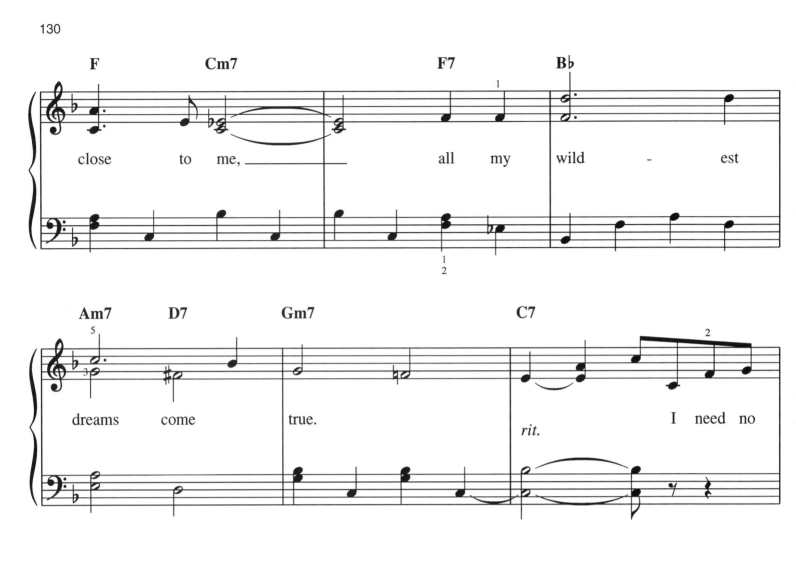

close to me, _____ all my wild - est

dreams come true. *rit.* I need no

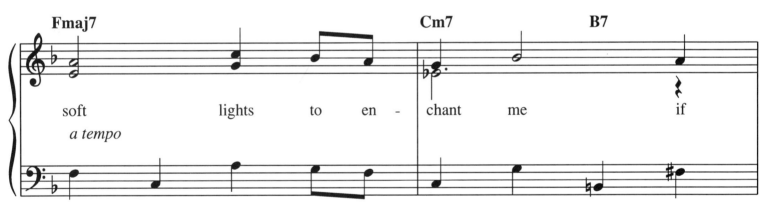

soft lights to en - chant me if

a tempo

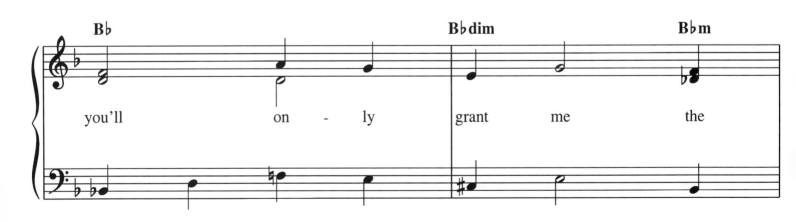

you'll on - ly grant me the

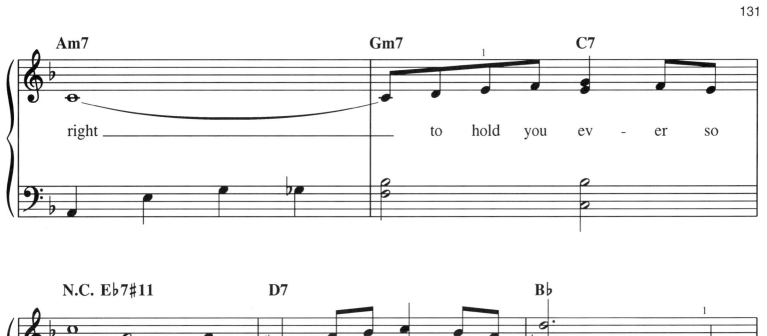

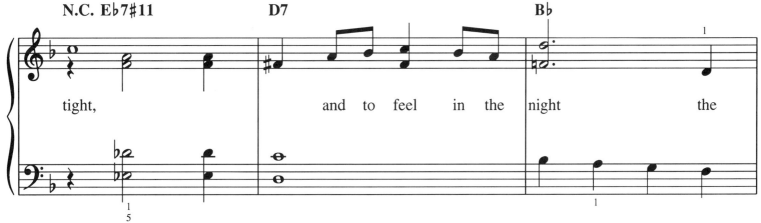

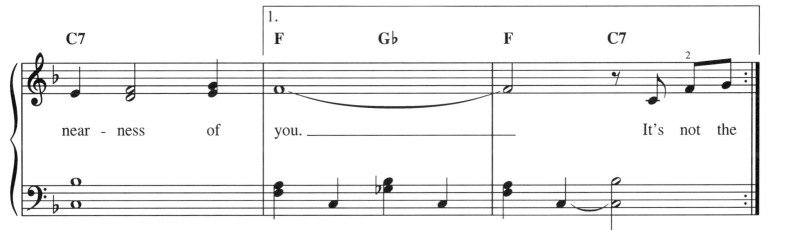

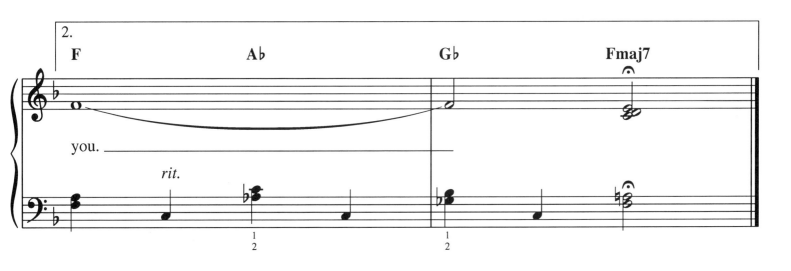

NEVER LET ME GO
from the Paramount Picture THE SCARLET HOUR

Words and Music by JAY LIVINGSTON
and RAY EVANS

Slowly and poignantly

Nev-er let me go,

love me much too much. If you let me go, life would lose its touch.

What would I be with-out you?___ There's no place for me with-

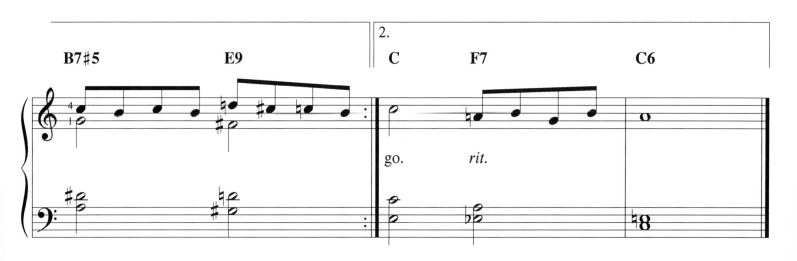

PICNIC
from the Columbia Technicolor Picture PICNIC

Words by STEVE ALLEN
Music by GEORGE W. DUNING

136

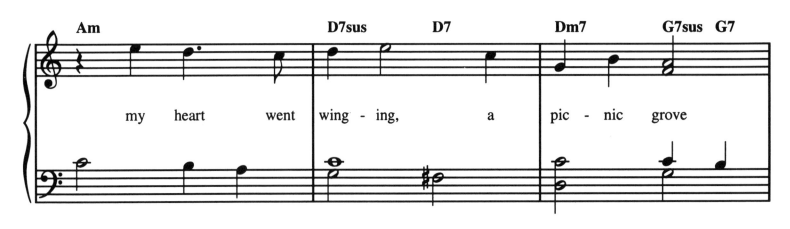

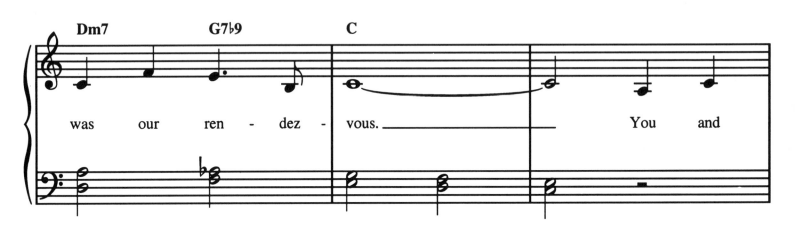

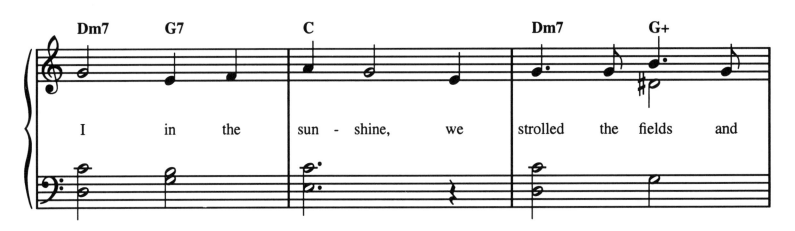

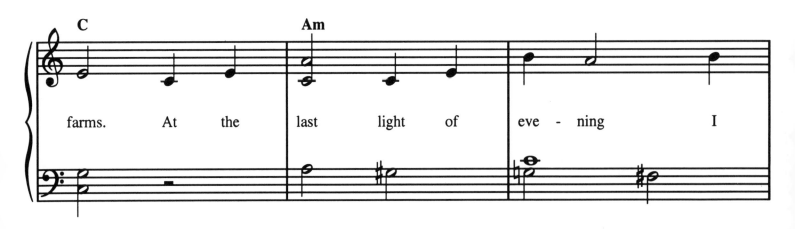

A NIGHTINGALE SANG IN BERKELEY SQUARE

Lyric by ERIC MASCHWITZ
Music by MANNING SHERWIN

140

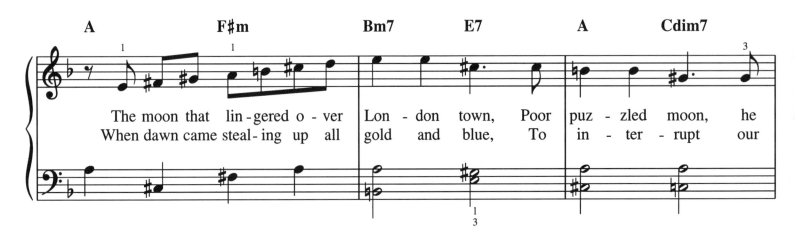

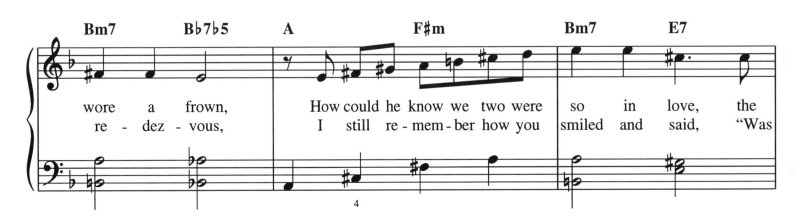

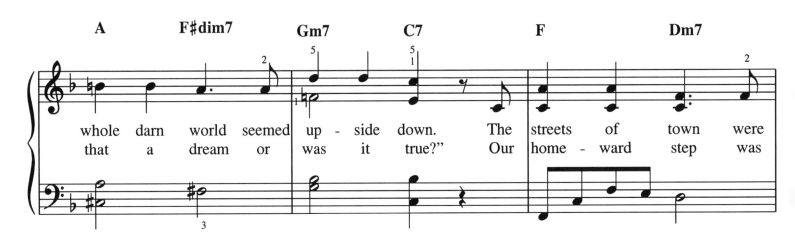

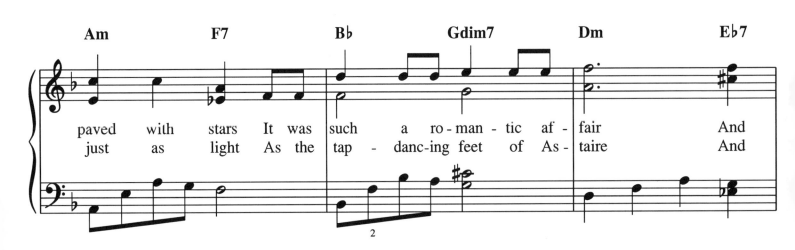

141

NOW IS THE HOUR

Words and Music by MAEWA KAIHAU,
CLEMENT SCOTT and DOROTHY STEWART

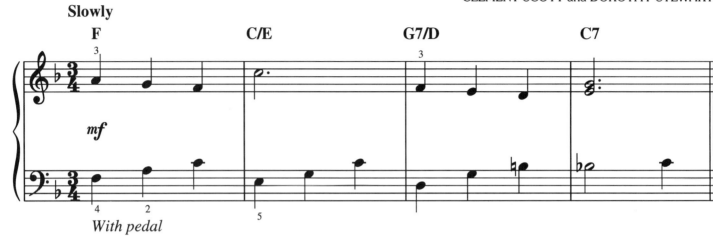

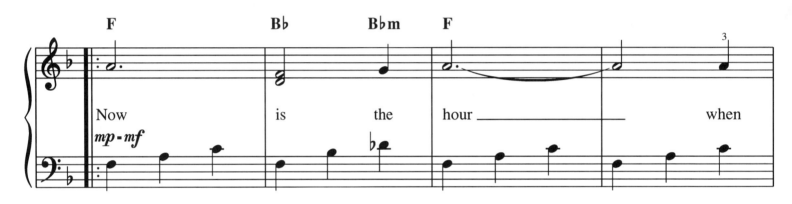

Now   is   the   hour _____   when

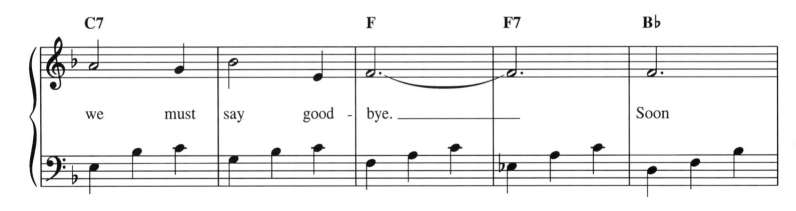

we   must   say   good - bye. _____   Soon

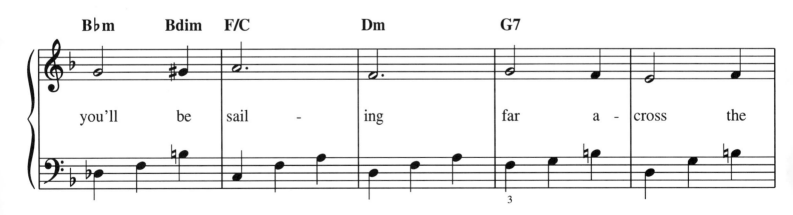

you'll   be   sail -   ing   far   a - cross   the

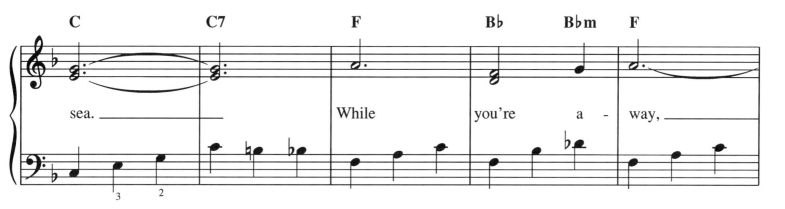

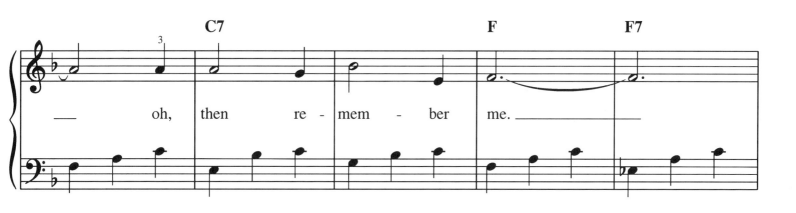

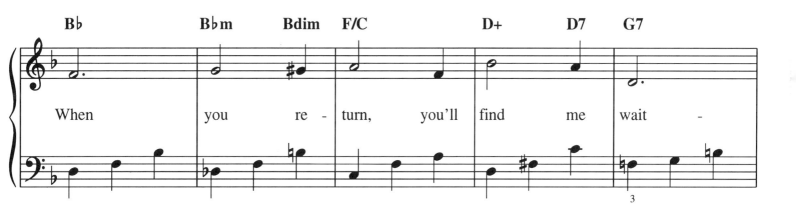

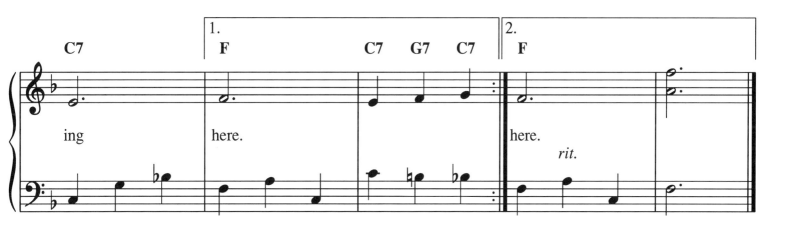

ONLY YOU
(And You Alone)

Words and Music by BUCK RAM
and ANDE RAND

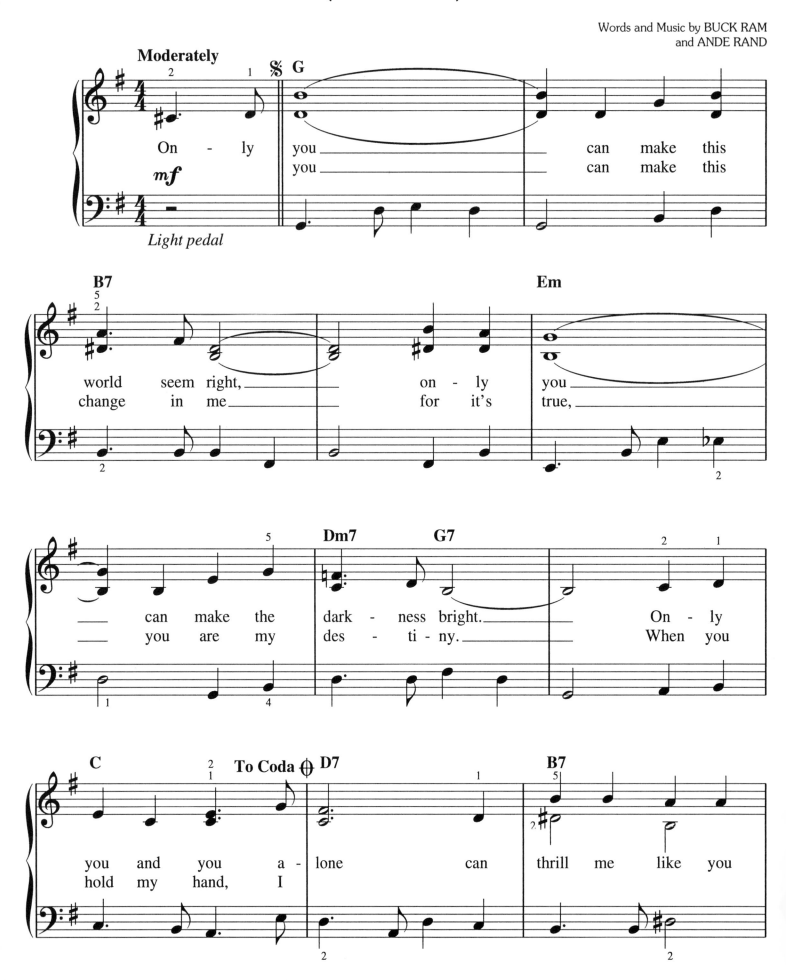

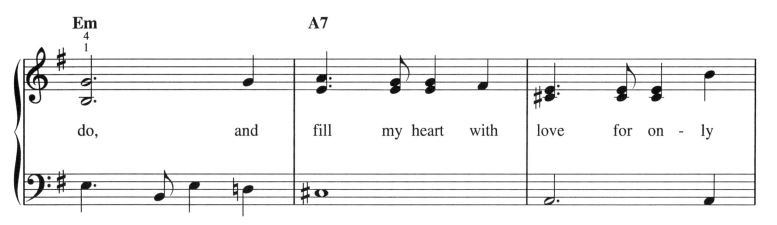

do, and fill my heart with love for on - ly

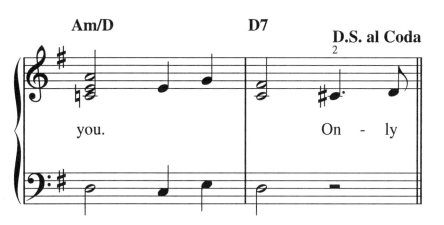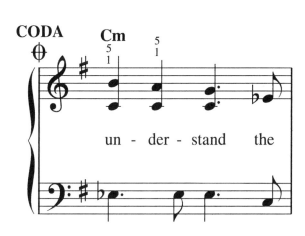

you. On - ly | un - der - stand the

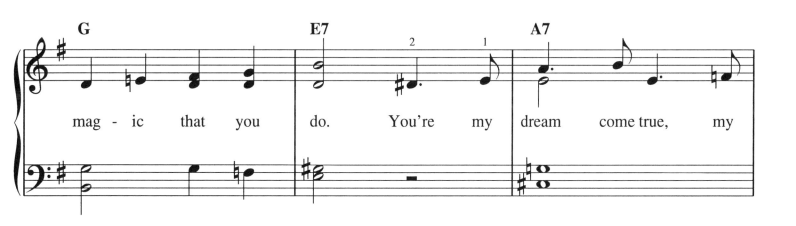

mag - ic that you do. You're my dream come true, my

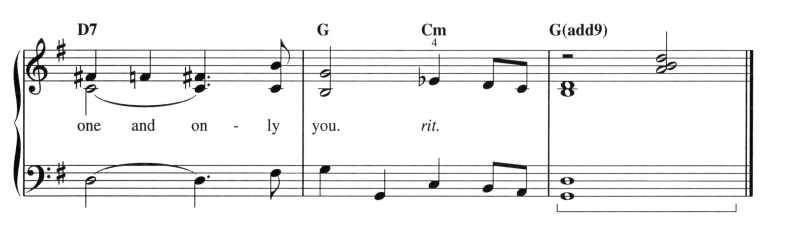

one and on - ly you. *rit.*

PEOPLE WILL SAY WE'RE IN LOVE

from OKLAHOMA!

Lyrics by OSCAR HAMMERSTEIN II
Music by RICHARD RODGERS

With a lilt

Don't throw bou - quets at me,
Don't sigh and gaze at me,

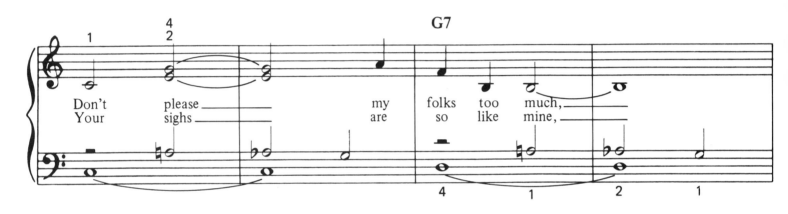

Don't please my folks too much,
Your sighs are so like mine,

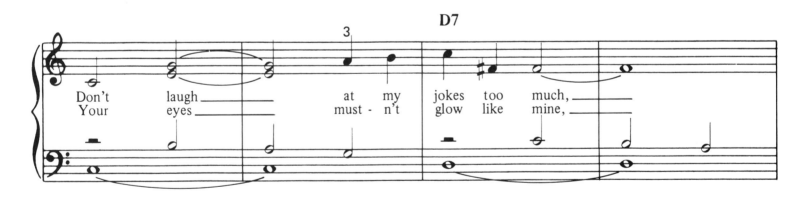

Don't laugh at my jokes too much,
Your eyes must - n't glow like mine,

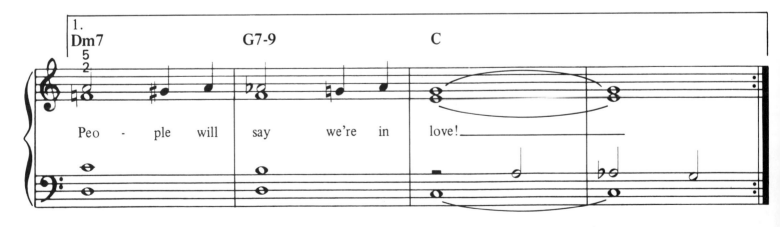

Peo - ple will say we're in love!

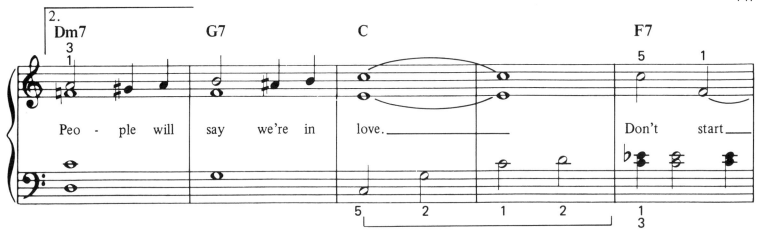

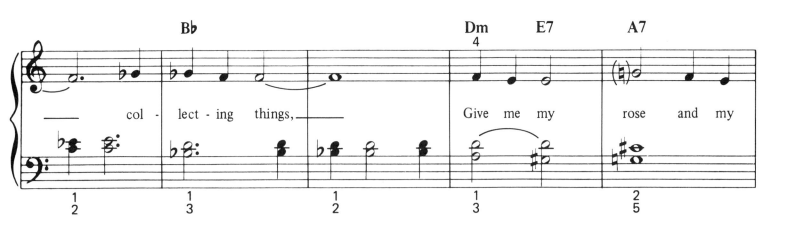

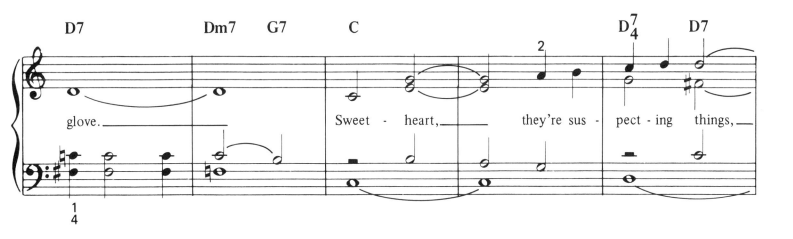

more deliberately

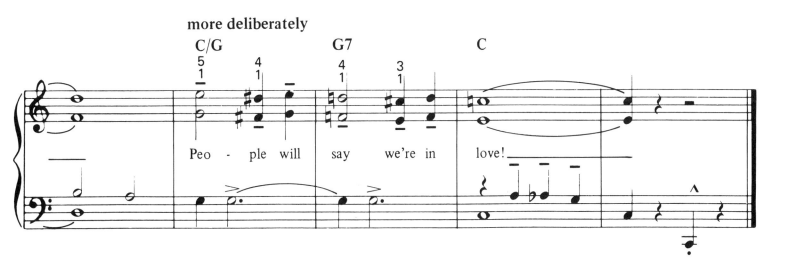

SEEMS LIKE OLD TIMES

from ARTHUR GODFREY AND HIS FRIENDS

Lyric and Music by JOHN JACOB LOEB
and CARMEN LOMBARDO

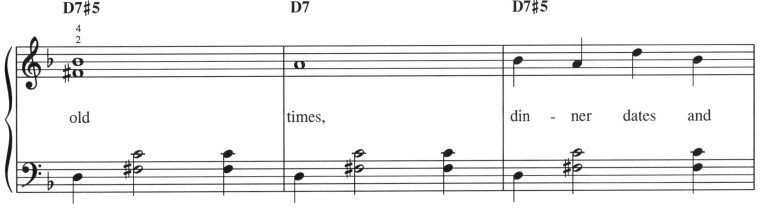

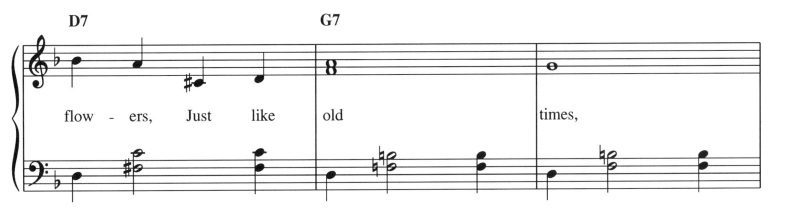

SINCE I DON'T HAVE YOU

Words and Music by JAMES BEAUMONT, JANET VOGEL,
JOSEPH VERSCHAREN, WALTER LESTER, LENNIE MARTIN,
JOSEPH ROCK and JOHN TAYLOR

Slowly

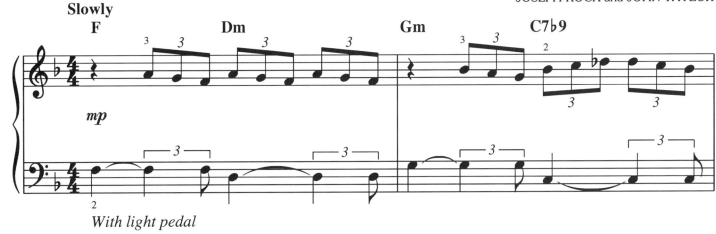

With light pedal

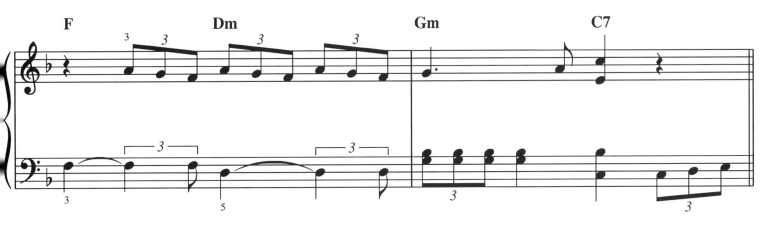

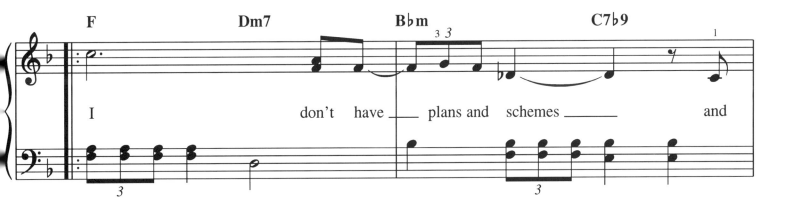

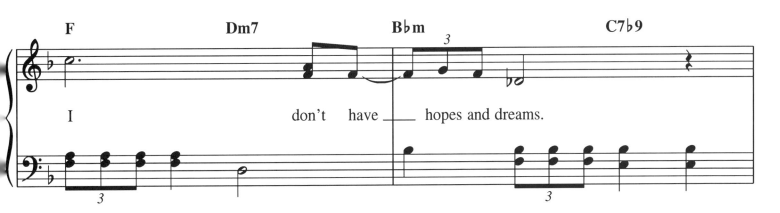

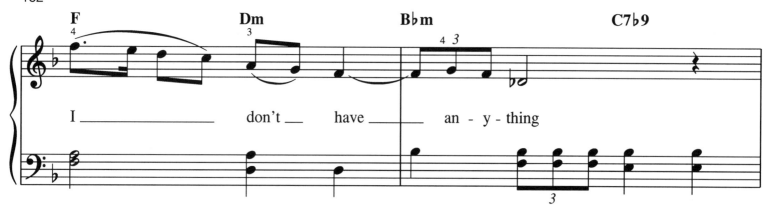

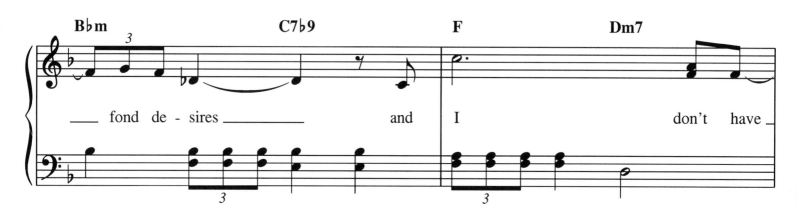

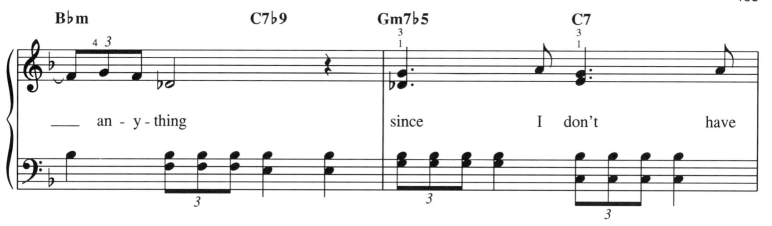

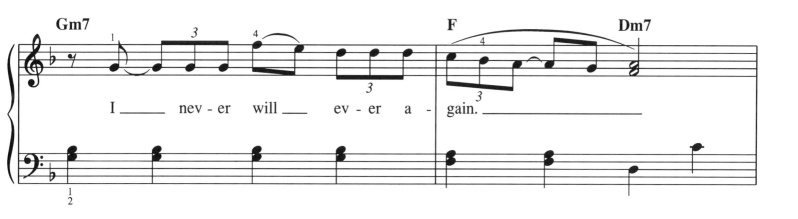

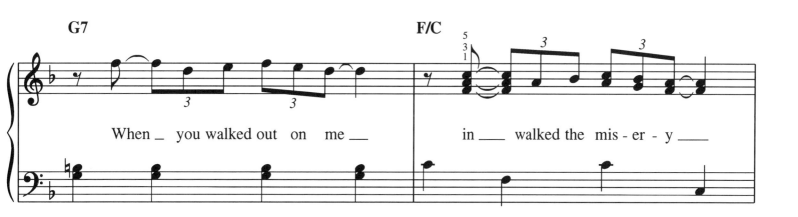

154

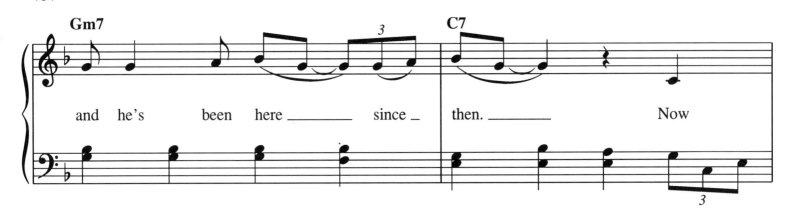

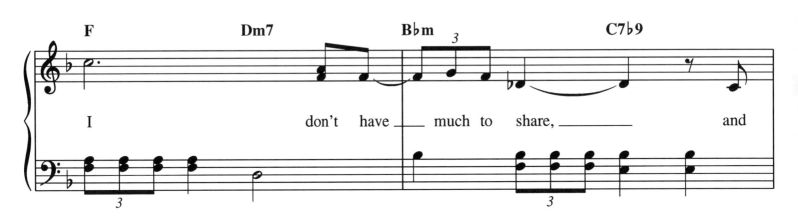

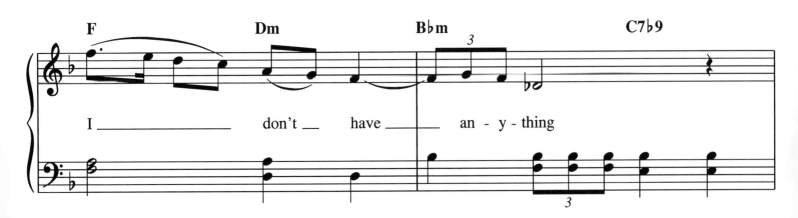

SO IN LOVE
from KISS ME, KATE

Words and Music by
COLE PORTER

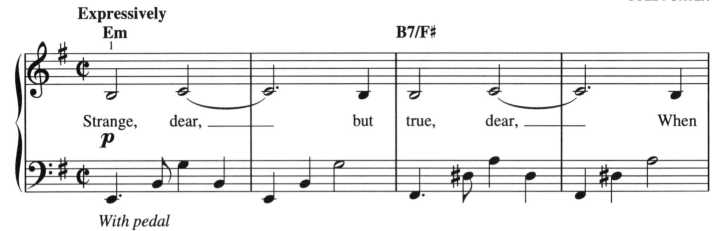

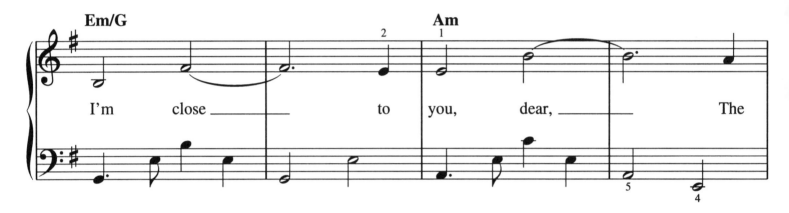

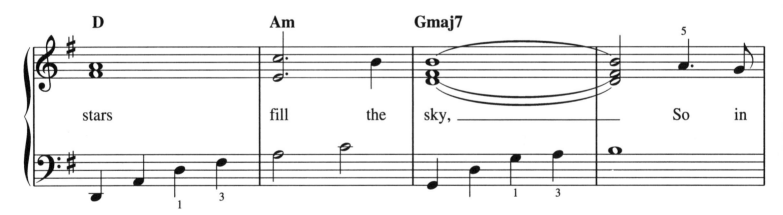

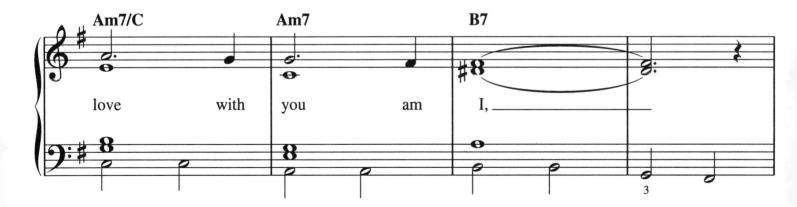

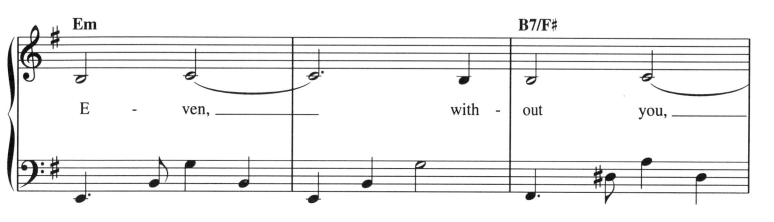

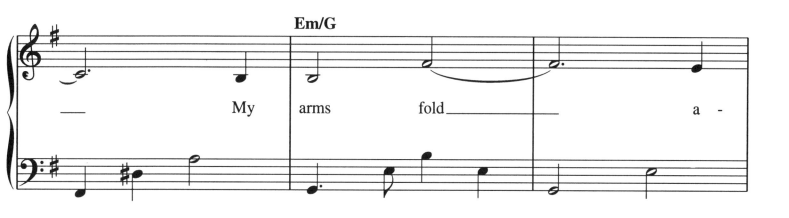

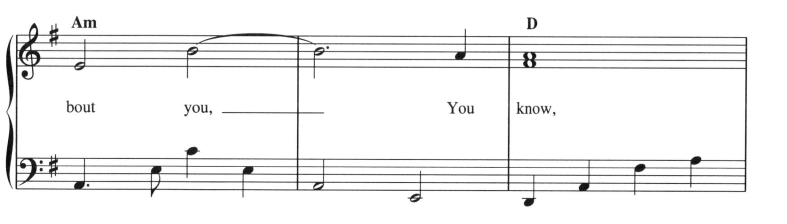

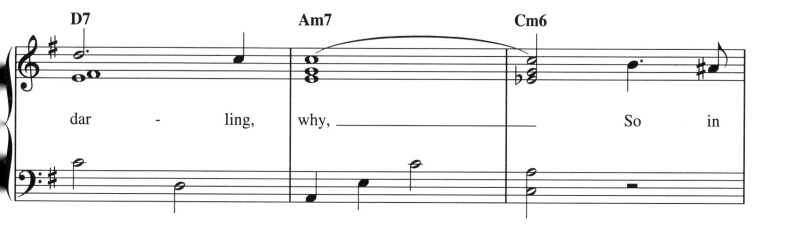

158

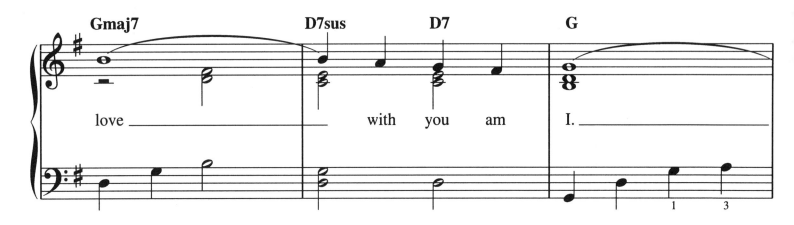

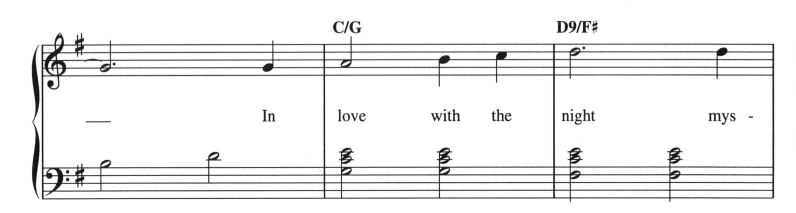

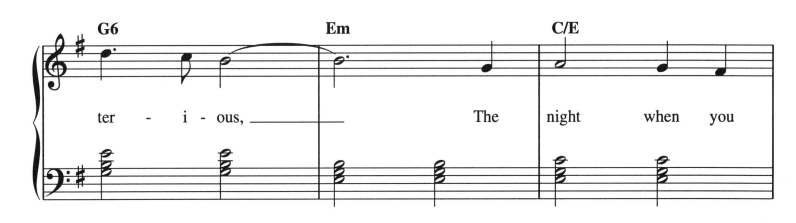

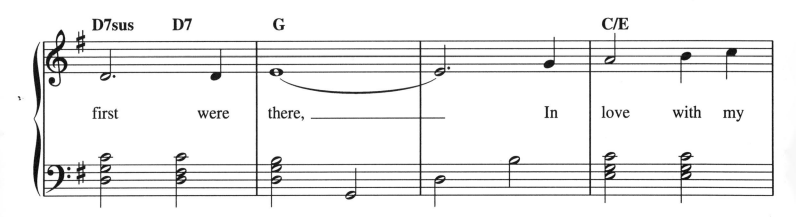

159

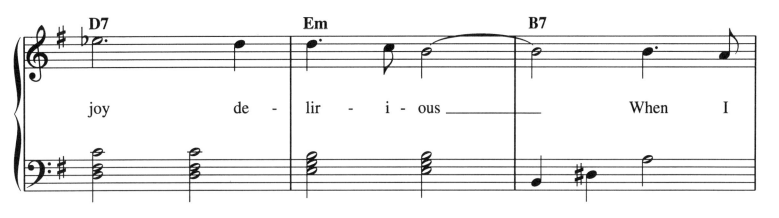

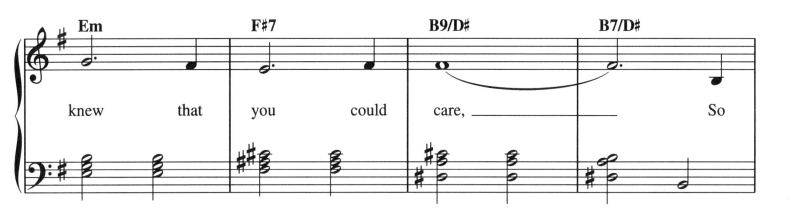

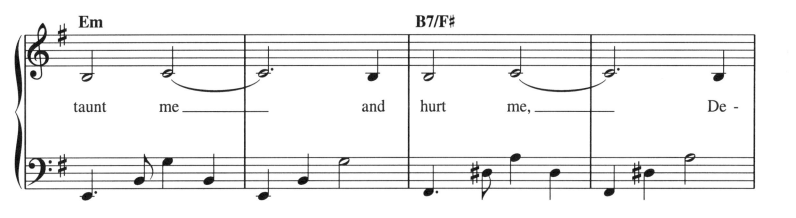

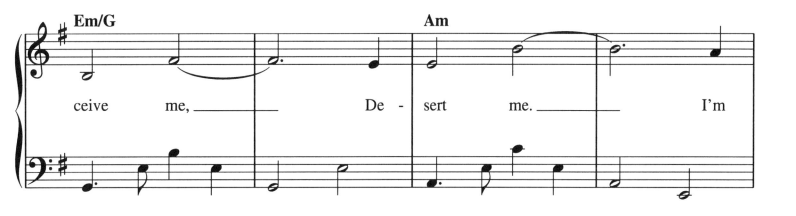

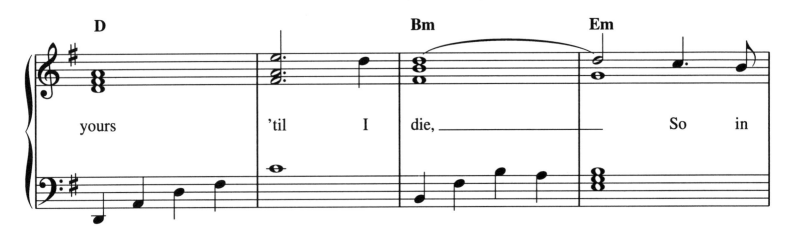
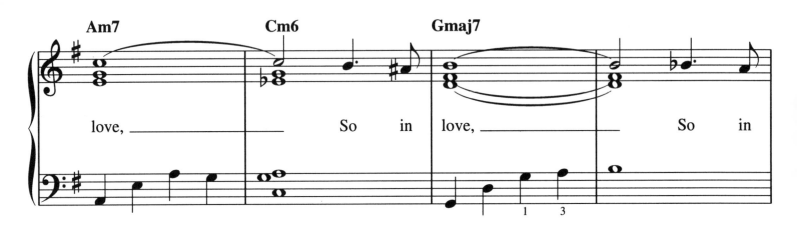
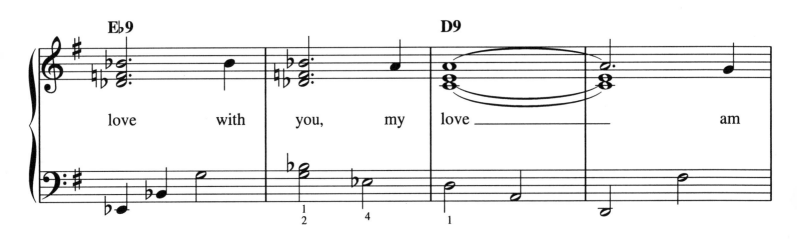
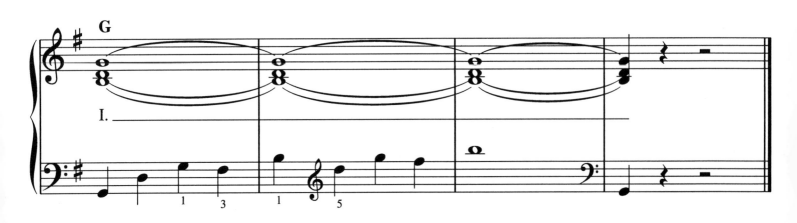

SUMMERTIME IN VENICE

from the Motion Picture SUMMERTIME

English Words by CARL SIGMAN
Music by ICINI

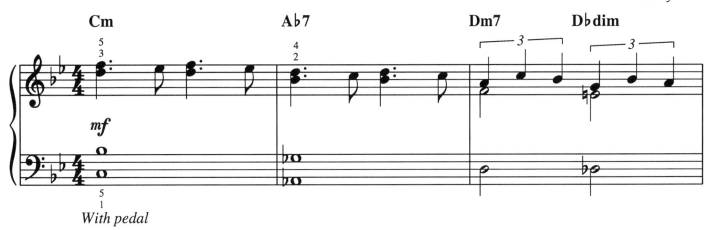

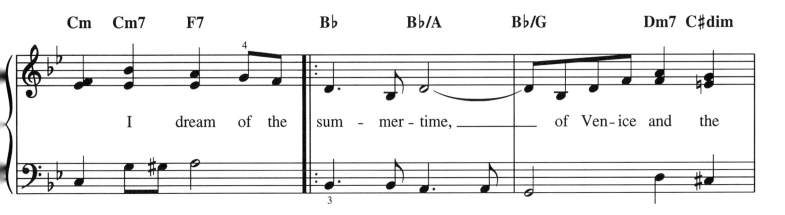

I dream of the sum-mer-time, _____ of Ven-ice and the

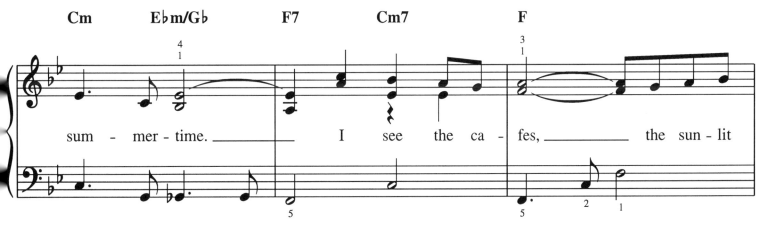

sum - mer - time. _____ I see the ca - fes, _____ the sun - lit

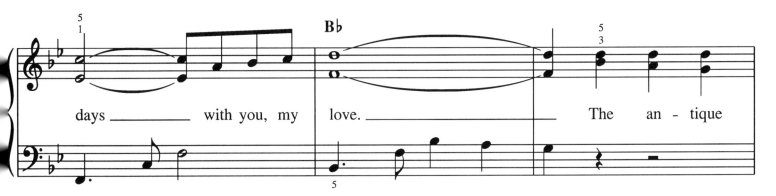

days _____ with you, my love. _____ The an - tique

162

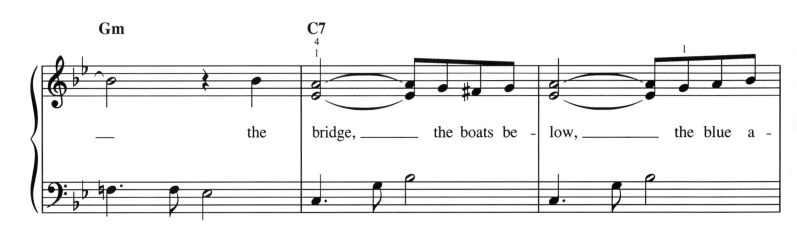

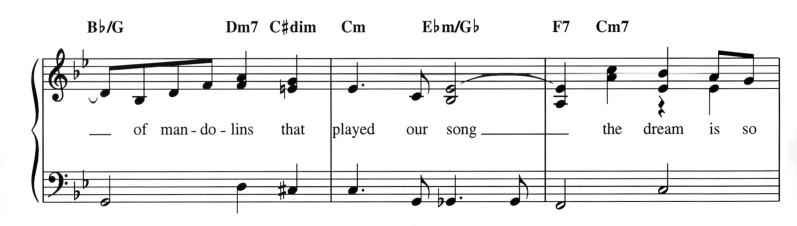

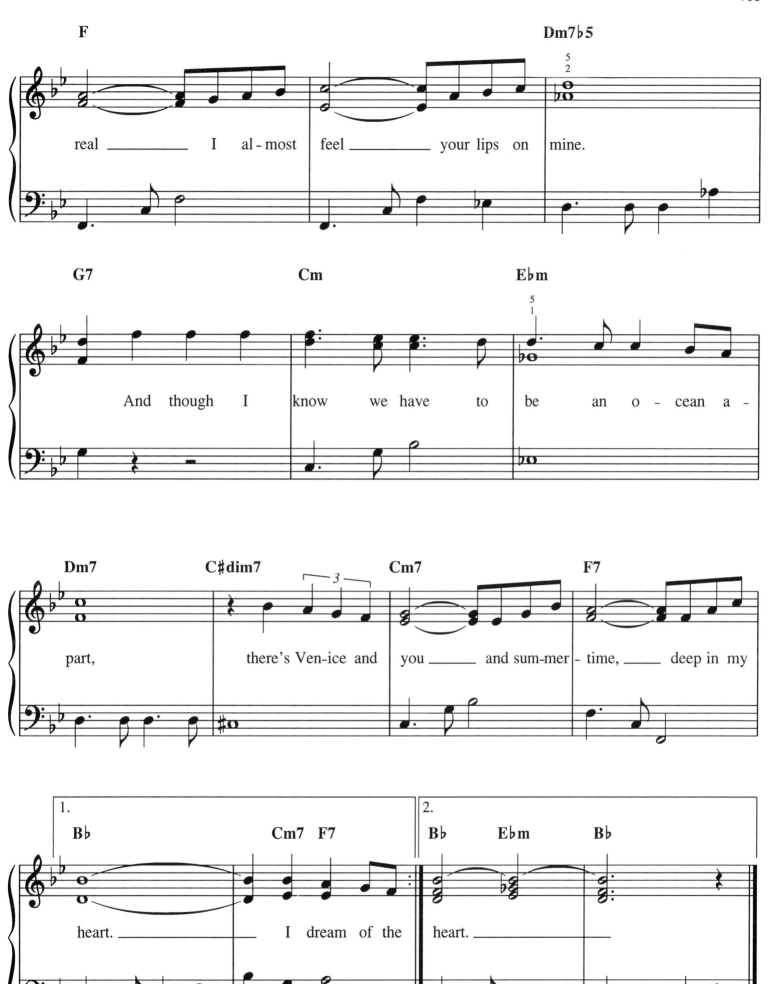

SOME ENCHANTED EVENING

from SOUTH PACIFIC

Lyrics by OSCAR HAMMERSTEIN II
Music by RICHARD RODGERS

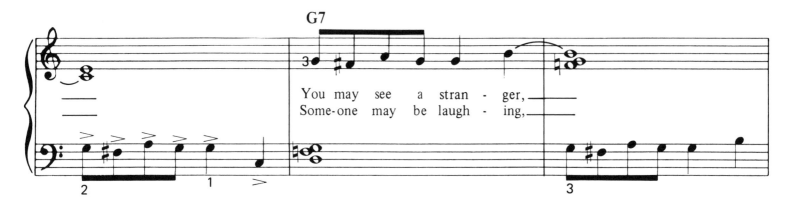

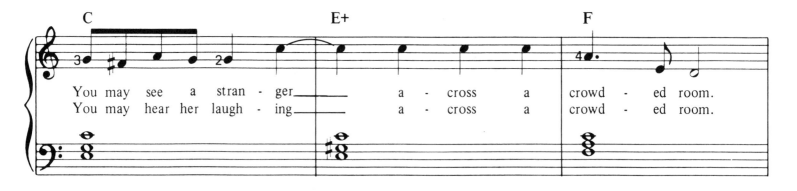

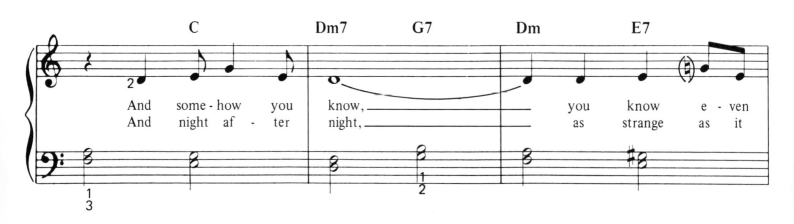

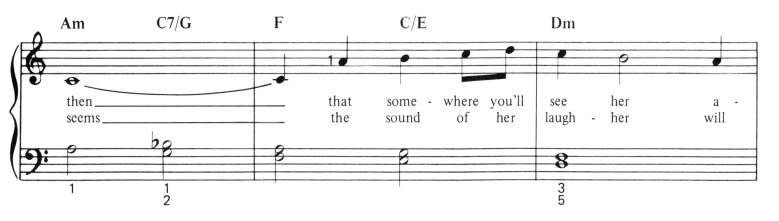

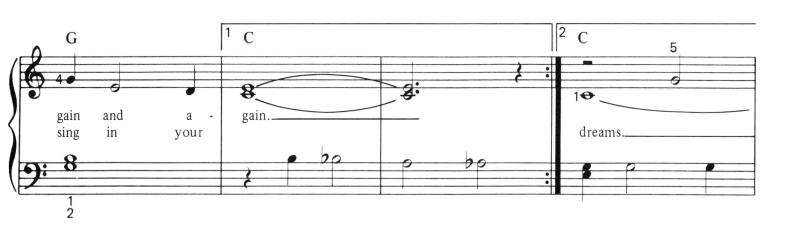

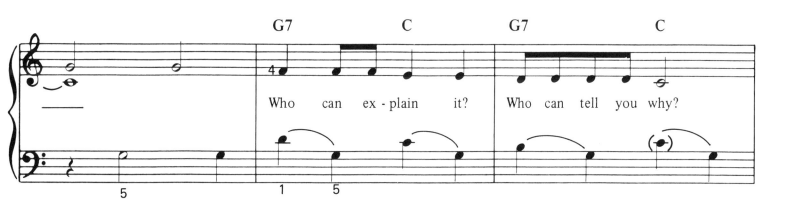

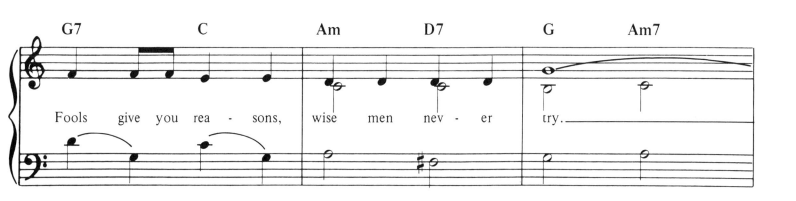

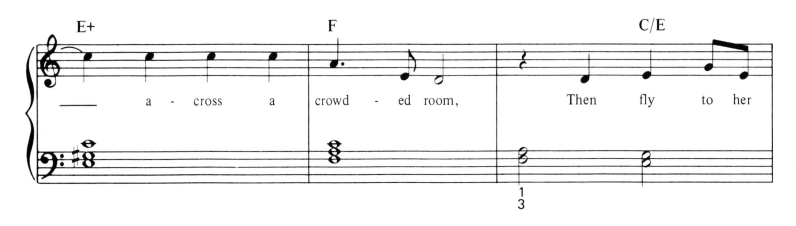

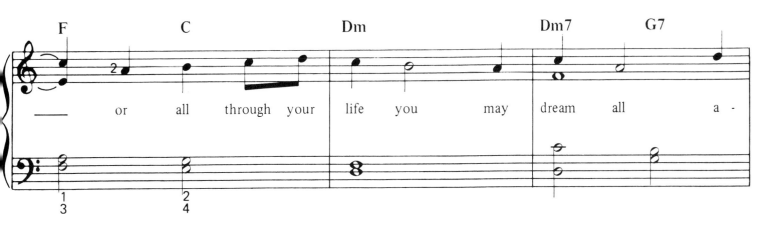

or all through your life you may dream all a-

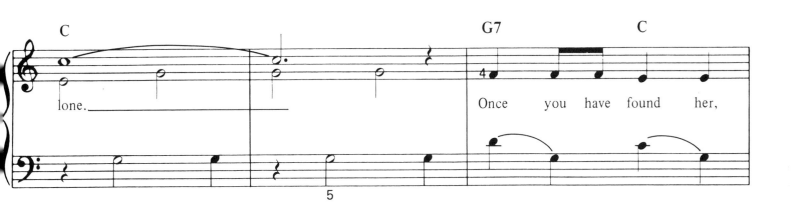

lone. Once you have found her,

nev - er let her go. Once you have found her nev - er

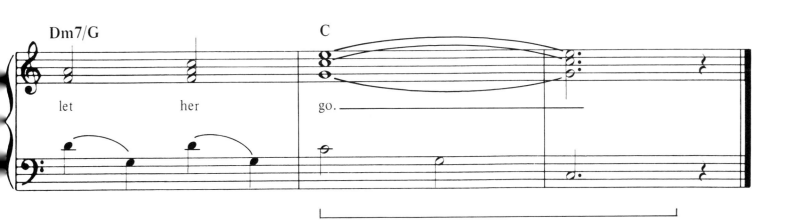

let her go.

STRANGER IN PARADISE

from KISMET

Words and Music by ROBERT WRIGHT
and GEORGE FORREST
(Music Based on Themes of A. BORODIN)

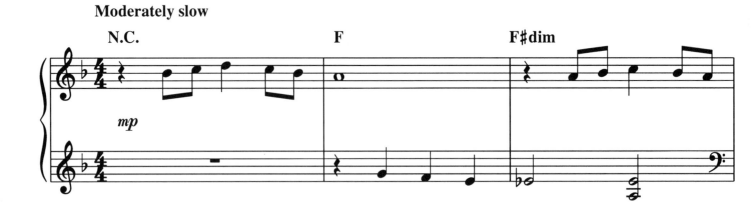

Take my hand, _____ I'm a stran - ger in par - a - dise,

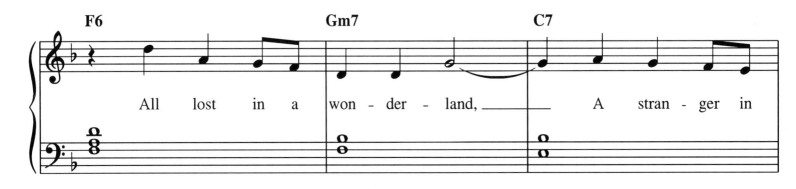

All lost in a won - der - land, _____ A stran - ger in

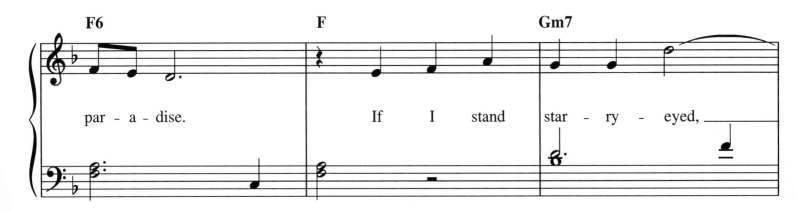

par - a - dise. If I stand star - ry - eyed, _____

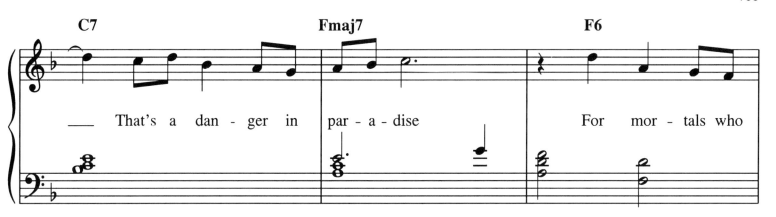

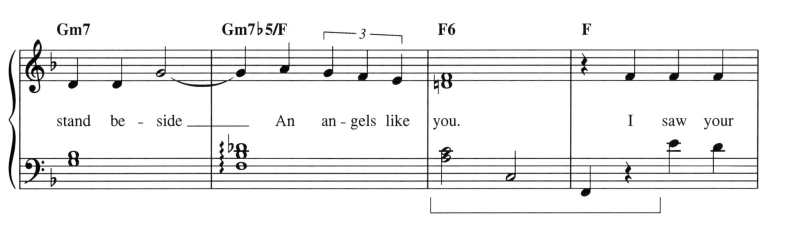

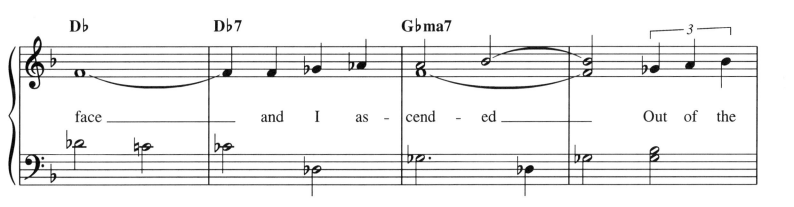

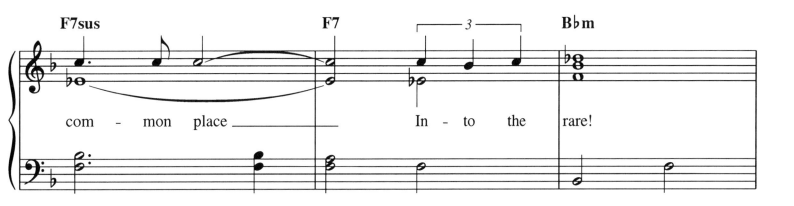

170

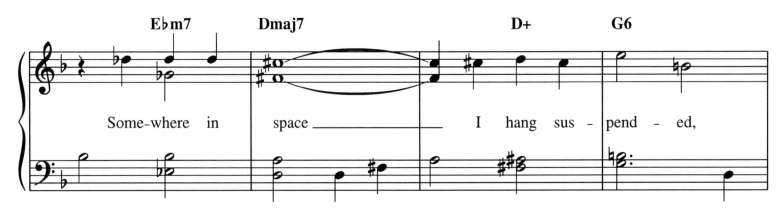

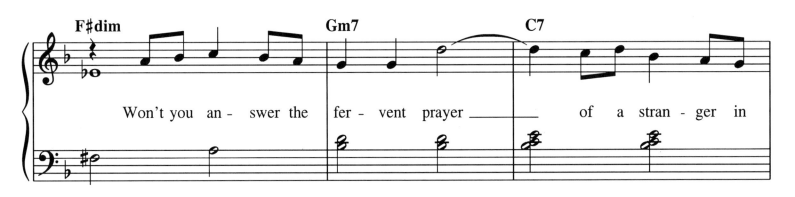

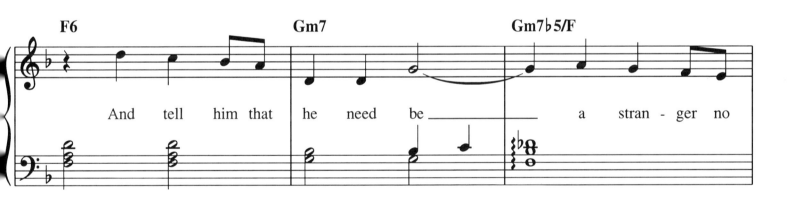

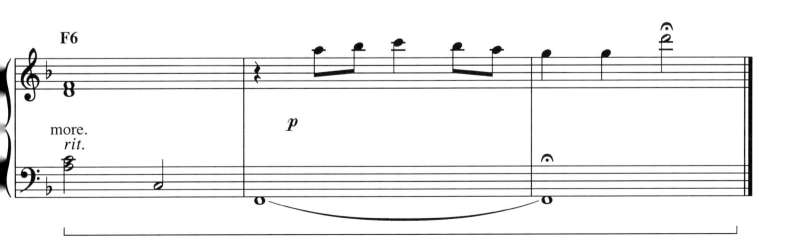

THAT OLD BLACK MAGIC

from the Paramount Picture STAR SPANGLED RHYTHM

Words by JOHNNY MERCER
Music by HAROLD ARLEN

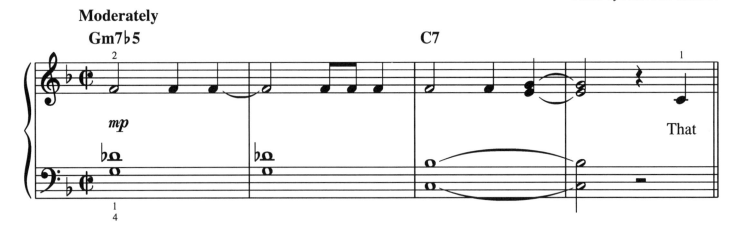

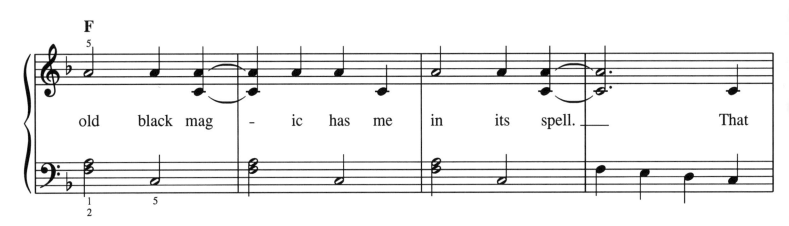

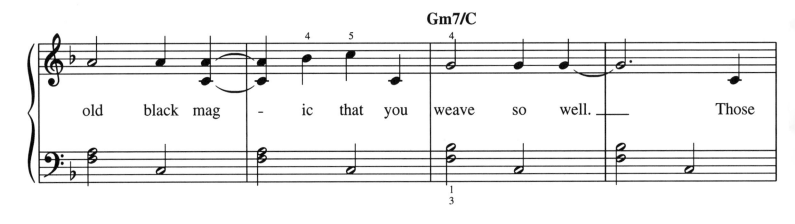

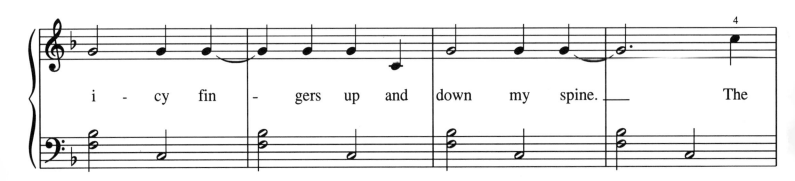

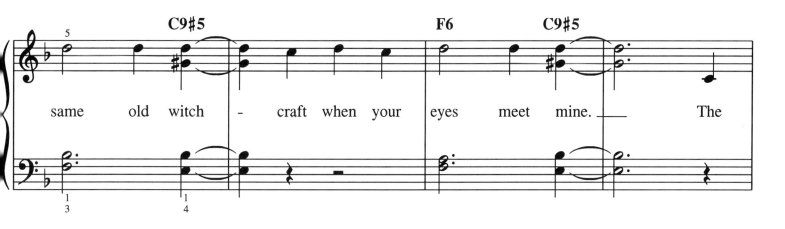

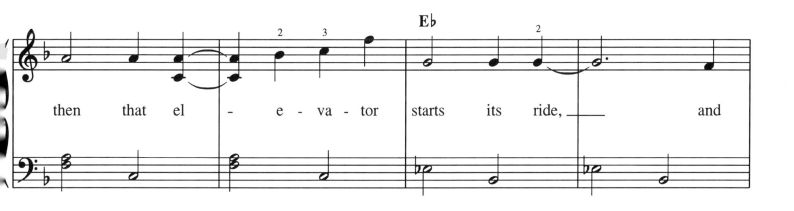

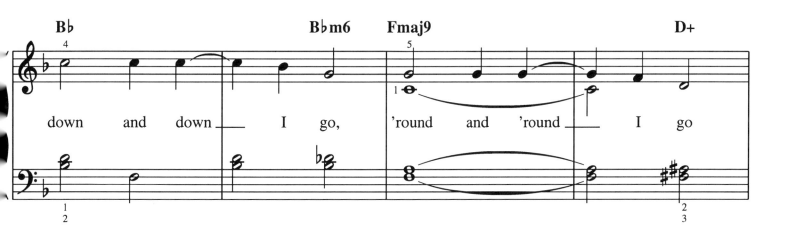

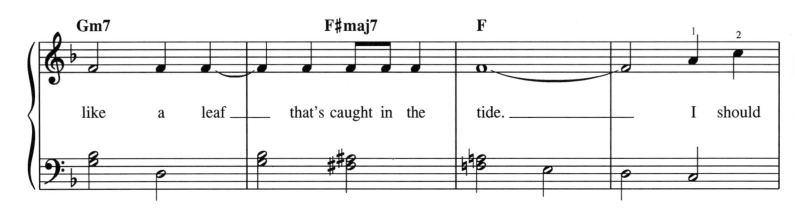

like a leaf ___ that's caught in the tide. ___ I should

stay a - way ___ but what can I do? ___

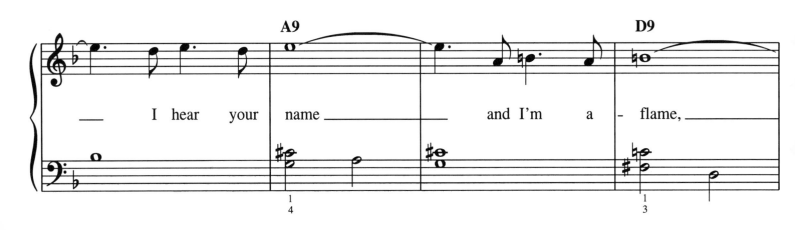

___ I hear your name ___ and I'm a - flame,

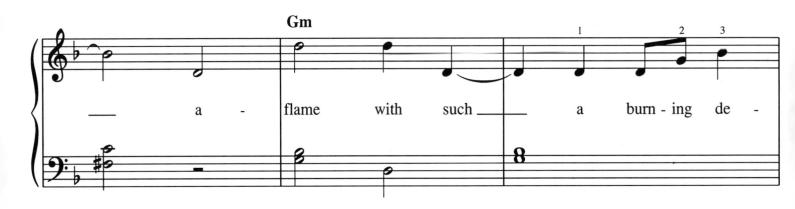

___ a - flame with such ___ a burn-ing de -

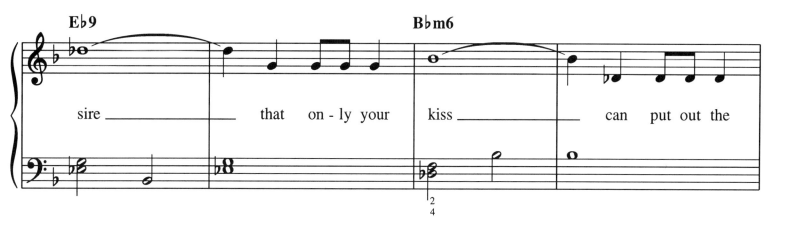

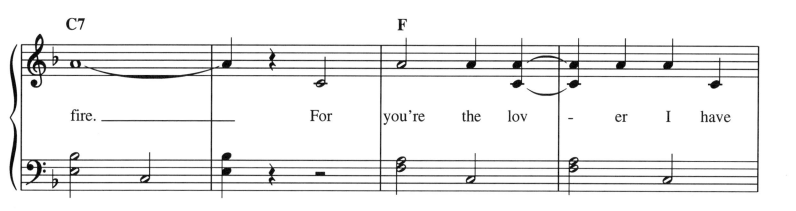

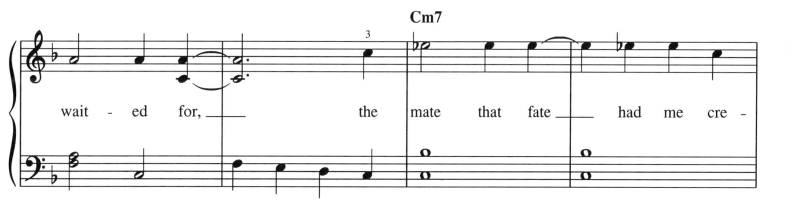

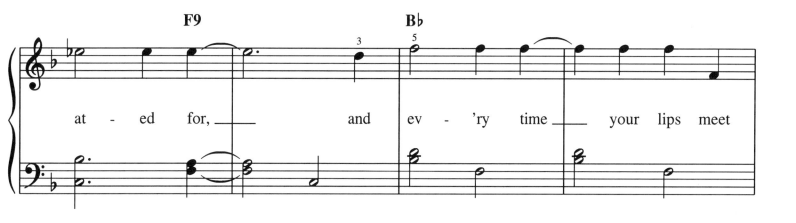

176

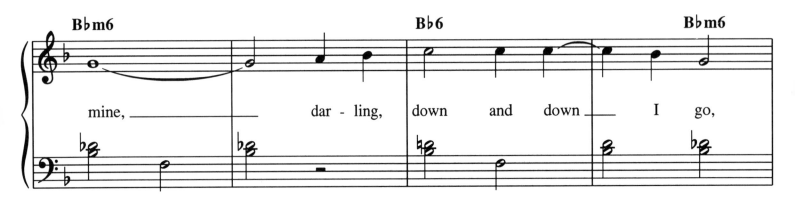

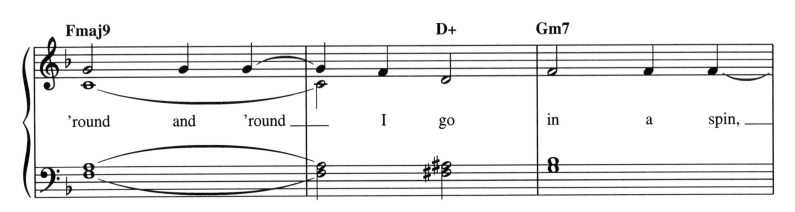

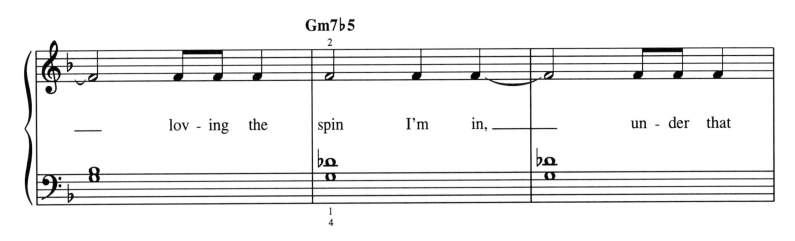

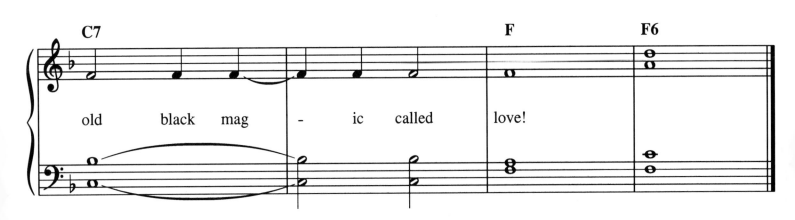

THEY SAY IT'S WONDERFUL
from the Stage Production ANNIE GET YOUR GUN

Words and Music by
IRVING BERLIN

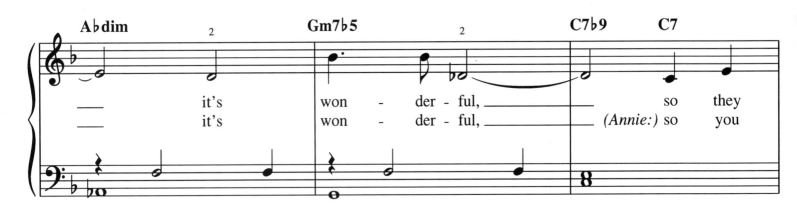

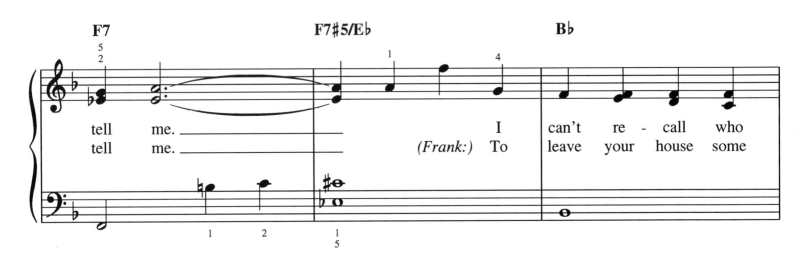

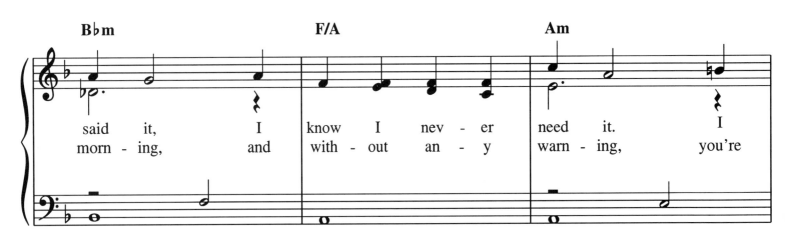

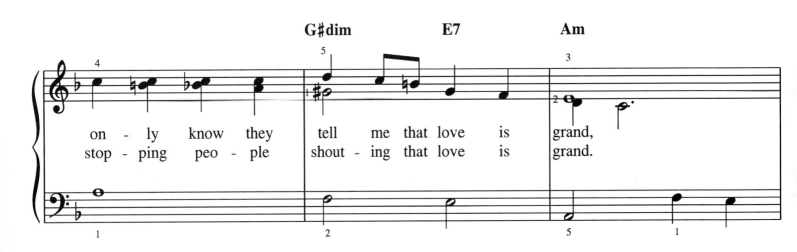

THAT'S AMORE
(That's Love)
from the Paramount Picture THE CADDY

Words by JACK BROOKS
Music by HARRY WARREN

When the moon hits your eye like a big piz - za pie, that's a - mor - é

When the world seems to shine like you've had too much wine, that's a - mor - é.

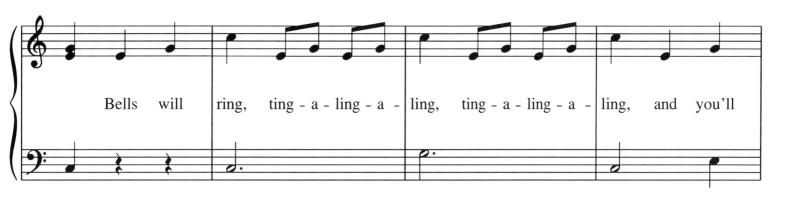

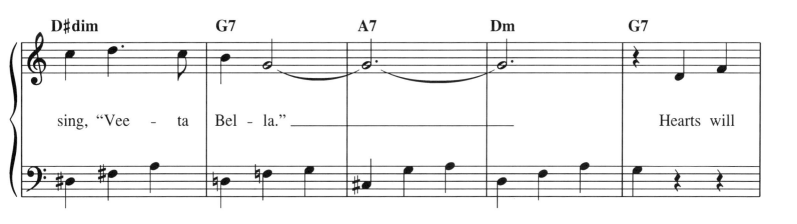

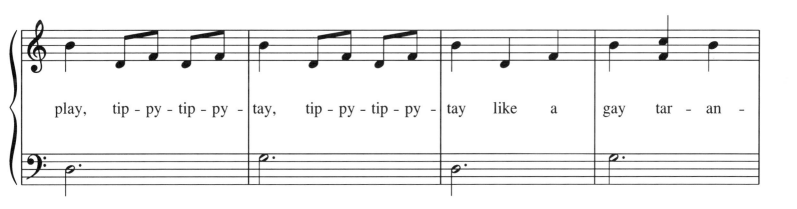

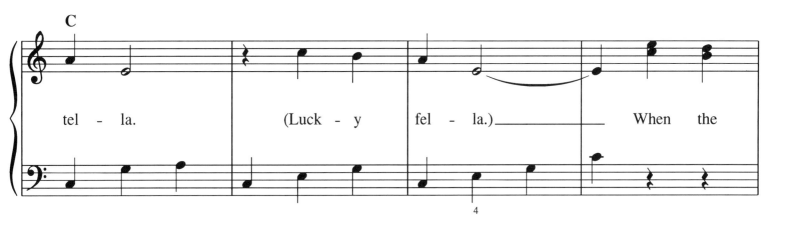

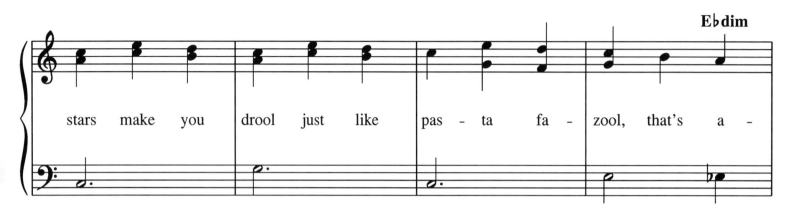

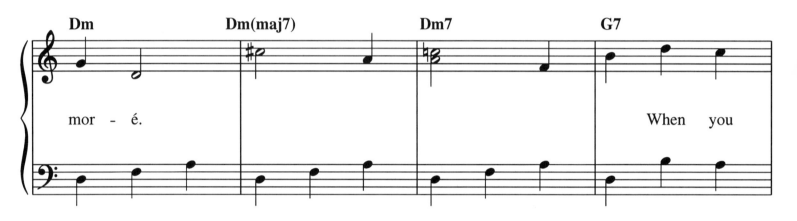

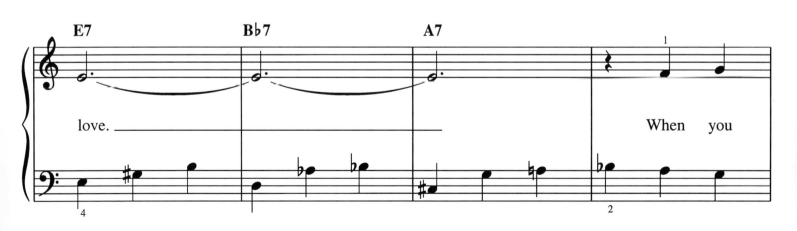

183

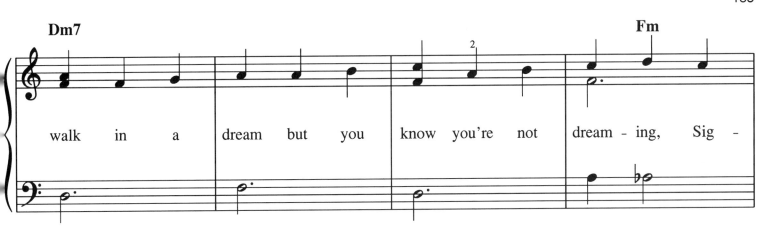

walk in a dream but you know you're not dream - ing, Sig -

nor - é. _____ Scuz - za

me, but you see, back in old Na - po - li, that's a -

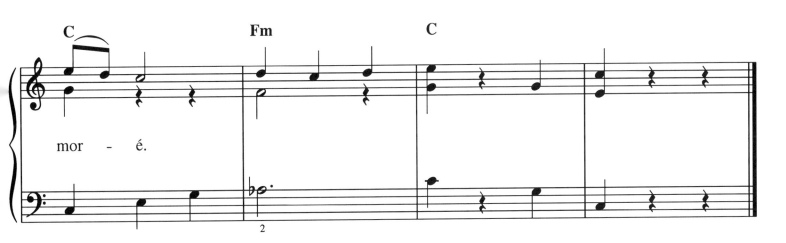

mor - é.

TRUE LOVE
from HIGH SOCIETY

Words and Music by
COLE PORTER

THREE COINS IN THE FOUNTAIN

Words by SAMMY CAHN
Music by JULE STYNE

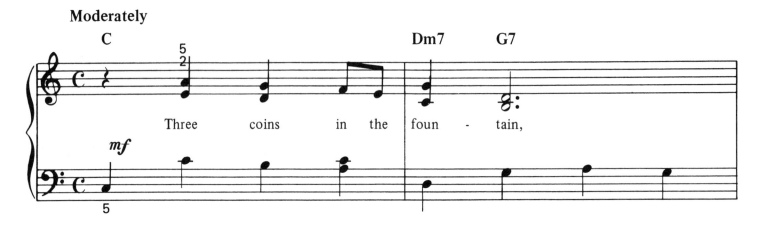

Three coins in the foun-tain,

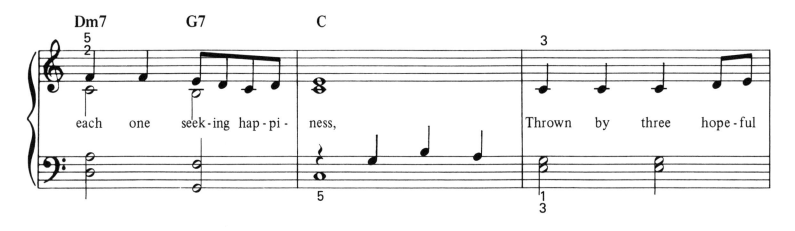

each one seek-ing hap-pi-ness,   Thrown by three hope-ful

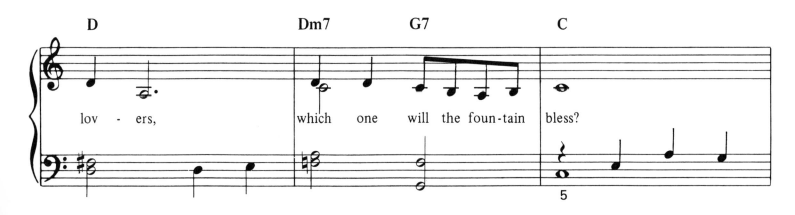

lov-ers,   which one will the foun-tain bless?

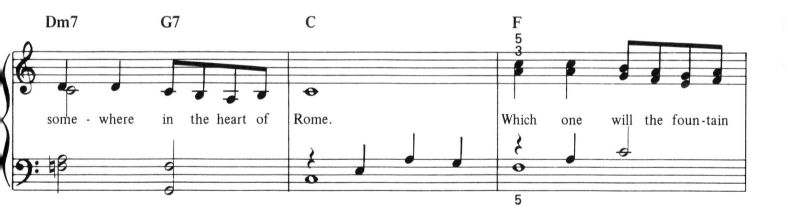

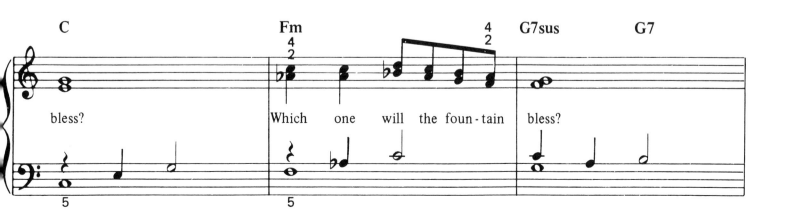

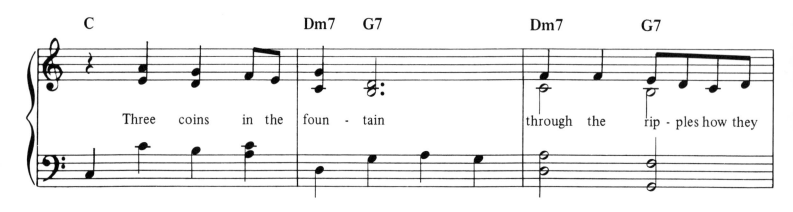

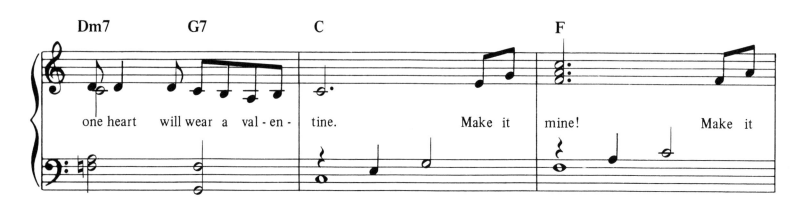

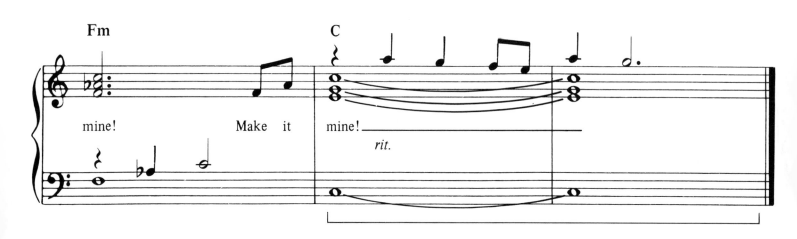

WHEN I FALL IN LOVE

from ONE MINUTE TO ZERO

Words by EDWARD HEYMAN
Music by VICTOR YOUNG

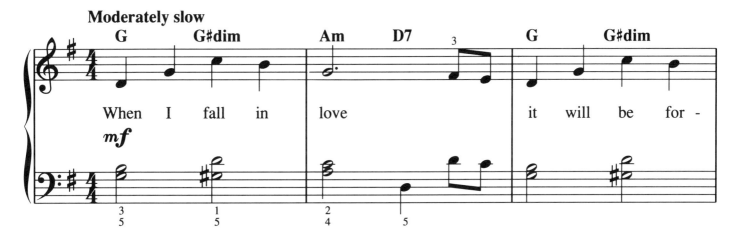

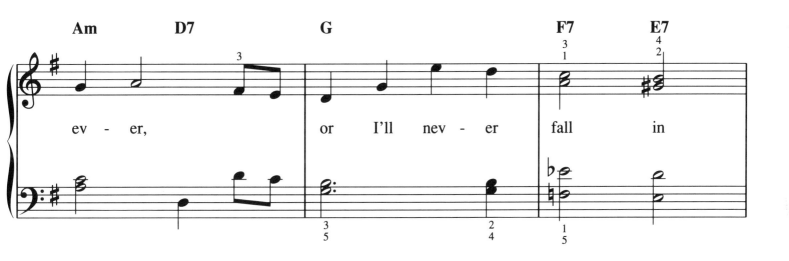

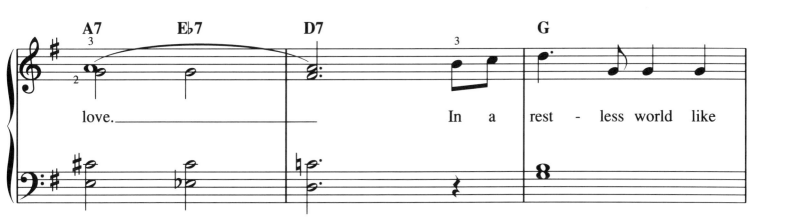

190

this is, love is end-ed be-fore it's be-gun, and too

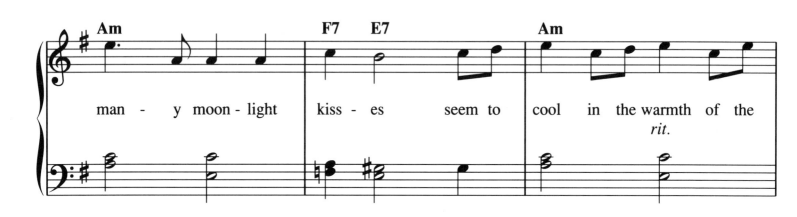

man - y moon-light kiss - es seem to cool in the warmth of the
rit.

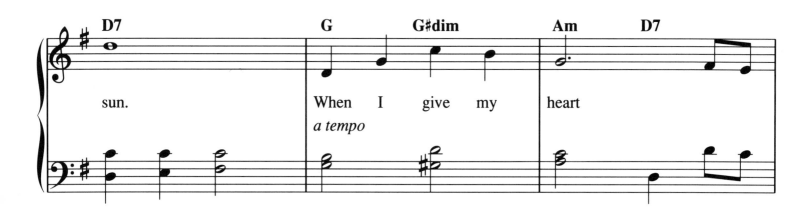

sun. When I give my heart
a tempo

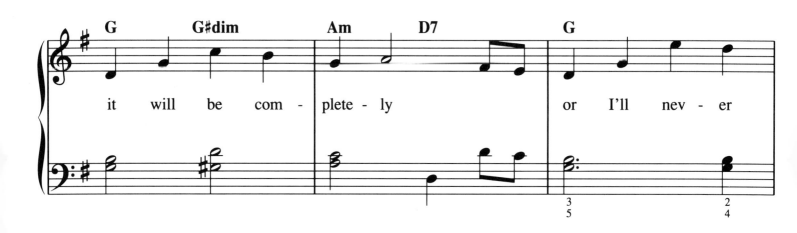

it will be com - plete-ly or I'll nev-er

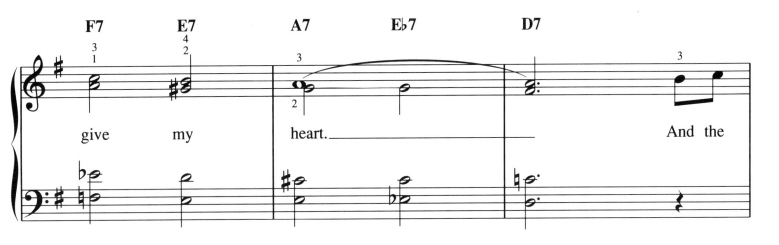

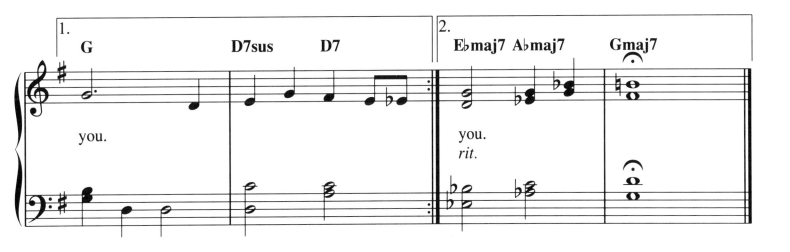

YOU ARE MY SUNSHINE

Words and Music by JIMMIE DAVIS
and CHARLES MITCHELL

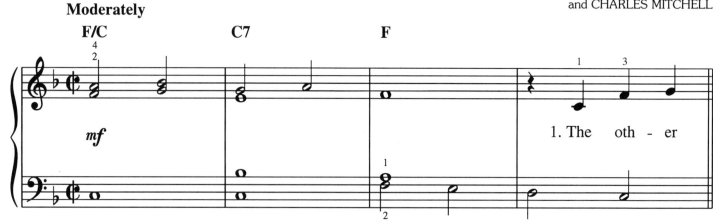

1. The oth - er

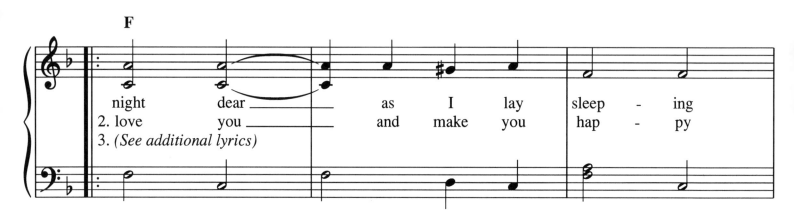

night dear _____ as I lay sleep - ing
2. love you _____ and make you hap - py
3. (See additional lyrics)

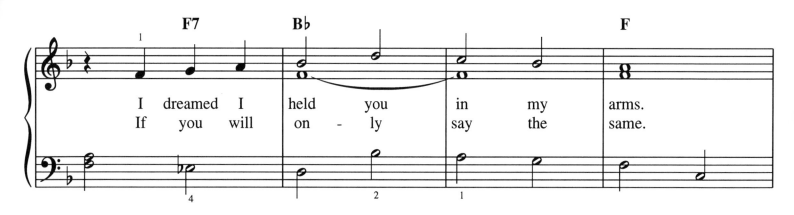

I dreamed I held you in my arms.
If you will on - ly say the same.

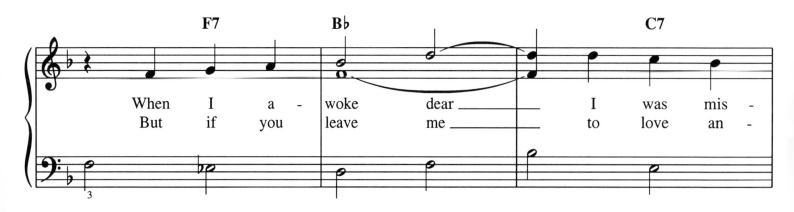

When I a - woke dear _____ I was mis -
But if you leave me _____ to love an -

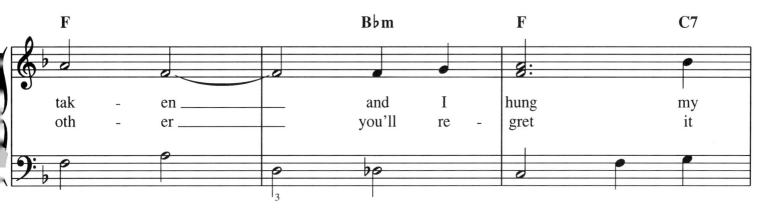

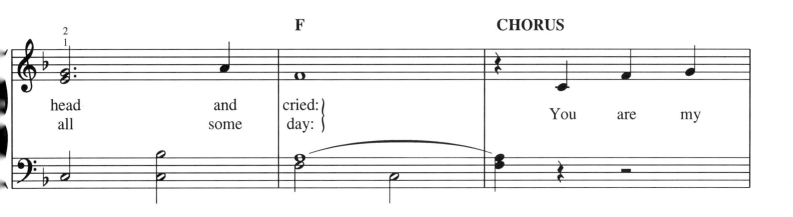

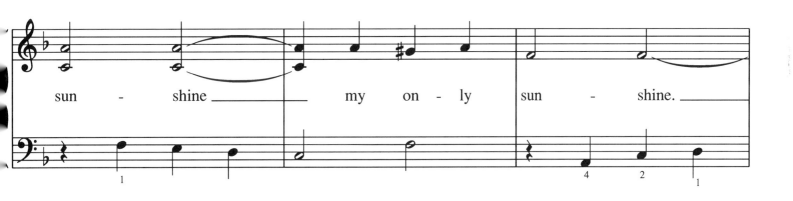

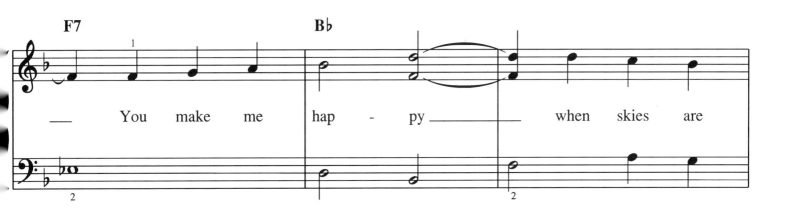

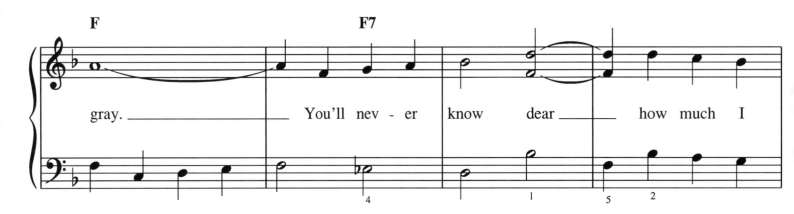

gray. _____ You'll nev - er know dear _____ how much I

love you. _____ Please don't take my sun - shine a -

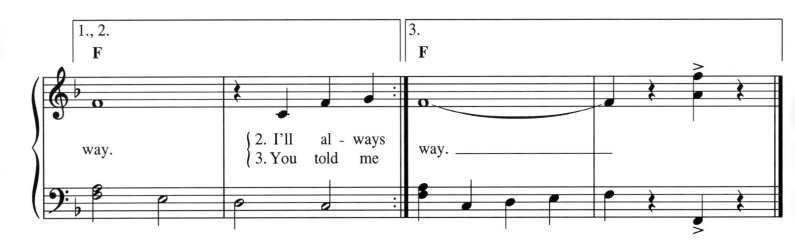

1., 2.
F
way.
2. I'll al - ways
3. You told me

3.
F
way. _____

Additional Lyrics

3. You told me once dear you really loved me
And no one else could come between.
But now you've left me and love another.
You have shattered all my dreams:
Chorus

YOU'RE NEARER
from TOO MANY GIRLS

Words by LORENZ HART
Music by RICHARD RODGERS

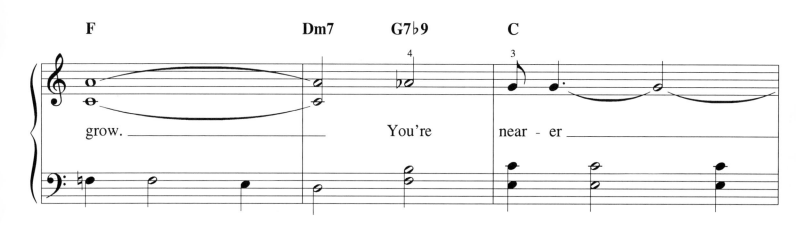

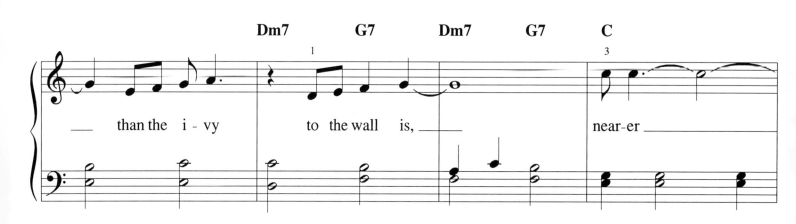

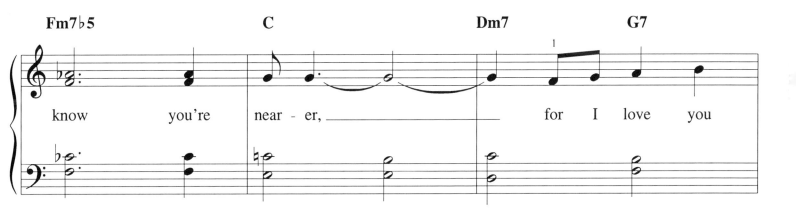

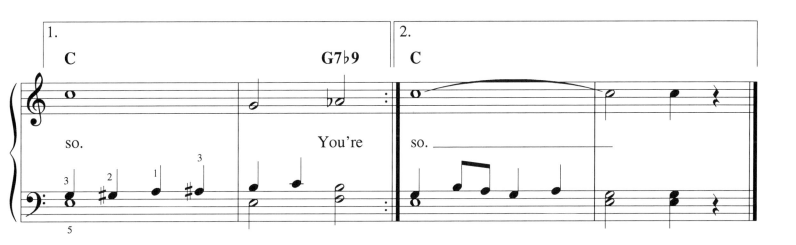

YOU'RE NOBODY 'TIL SOMEBODY LOVES YOU

Words and Music by RUSS MORGAN,
LARRY STOCK and JAMES CAVANAUGH

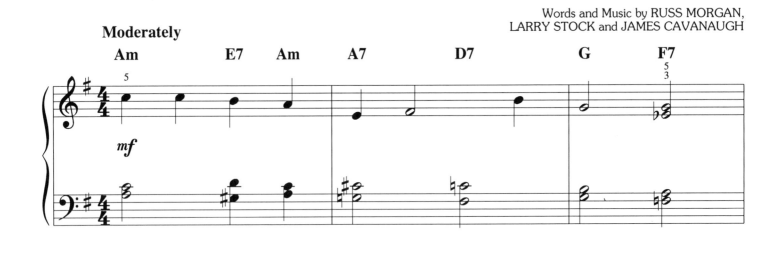

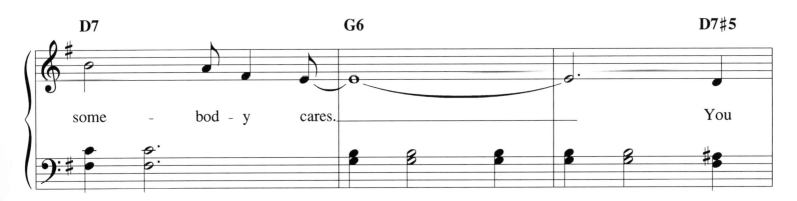

may be king, __ you may pos - sess __ the world and its gold.

__ But gold won't bring __ you hap - pi - ness __ when

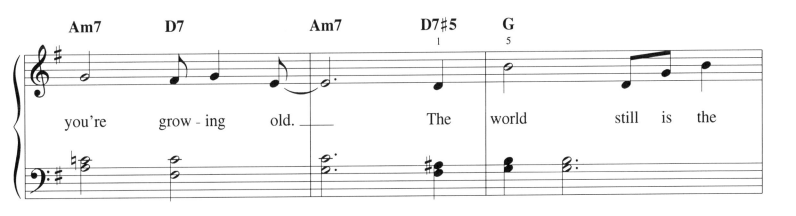

you're grow - ing old. __ The world still is the

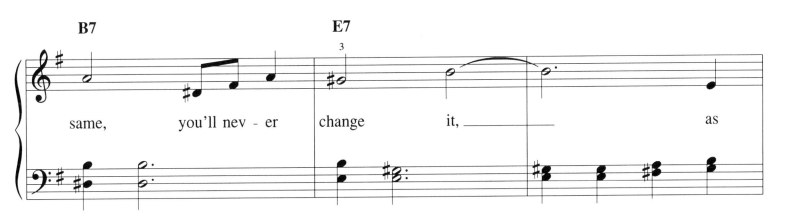

same, you'll nev - er change it, __ as

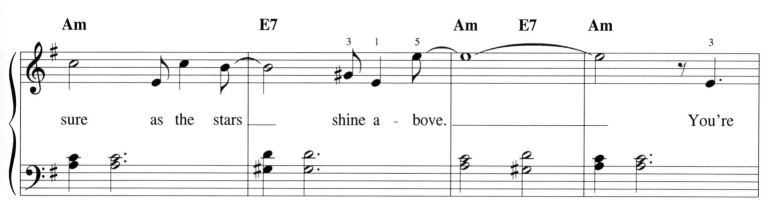

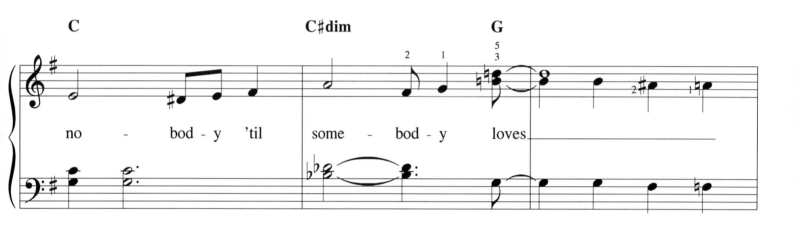

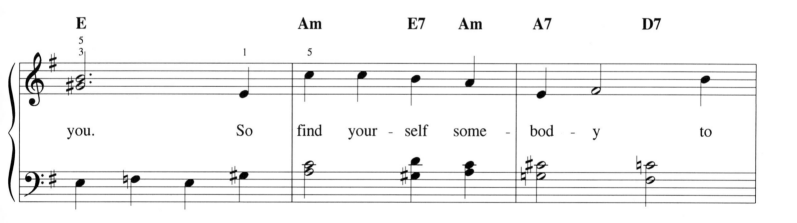